W9-AVJ-242

101 Things to Do
Before You're
Old and Boring

Dedicated to

Christine and Neville, Clarissa and George

and everyone else's

	and	
*		*

* Write your own dedications in here

Dedicated to
Christine and Neville, Clarissa and George
and everyone else's
Mom and Dad

Copyright © 2005 by Richard Horne and Helen Szirtes

All rights reserved. No part of this book may be reproduced or transmitted in any form or by
any means, electronic or mechanical, including photocopying, recording, or by any information
storage and retrieval system, without permission in writing from the publisher.

First published in the United States of America in 2006 by
Walker Publishing Company, Inc.
Distributed to the trade by Holtzbrinck Publishers

First published in Great Britain in 2005 by Bloomsbury Publishing Plc

For information about permission to reproduce selections from
this book, write to Permissions, Walker & Company,
104 Fifth Avenue, New York, New York 10011

Library of Congress Cataloging-in-Publication Data available
upon request
ISBN-10: 0-8027-7745-7 • ISBN-13: 978-0-8027-7745-4 (paperback)

Book design by Richard Horne

Visit Walker & Company's Web site at www.walkeryoungreaders.com

Printed in Tien Wah in Malaysia

4 6 8 10 9 7 5

All papers used by Walker & Company are natural, recyclable products
made from wood grown in well-managed forests. The manufacturing processes
conform to the environmental regulations of the country of origin.

www.101thingstodobook.com

101 Things to Do Before You're Old and Boring

Designed and illustrated by Richard Horne
Written by Richard Horne and Helen Szirtes

Walker & Company
New York

Introduction

Certain things in life are guaranteed. Firstly, we will get old, and secondly, without realizing it, we'll probably become boring too. Surely you've noticed how much time old people happily spend talking about when they were young? Well, this book offers a way to ensure that you also have hundreds of great memories to sustain you and plenty to talk about when you become old and boring. If you don't do these things now, the chances are you never will. So best get going before it's too late.

Attempt

Send a message in a bottle, bury a time capsule, make your own T-shirts and buttons, create a unique milk shake, start a new trend, learn to do something that no one else can do, invent a secret code, hide treasure and leave a map for someone to find, and much, much more....

Complete

Keep track of your achievements by filling in the easy-to-follow forms.

Become Old and Boring

When you're old and boring, look back at this book and bask in the glory of all the things you accomplished when you were young and exciting.

How to Use This Book

The idea is simple. Complete the **101 Things to Do** before you're old and boring, check the boxes, fill in the forms, and stick in the colored stars as you go.

About the Forms

- Be honest with the information you enter in the forms.
- You may find some of the forms too small for all the information you'd like to enter. To solve this problem, you can copy the extra pages at the back of the book or visit the website for extra or duplicate pages at **www.101thingstodobook.com**

Your **Things to Do**

If there are **Things to Do** you'd like to have a go at that aren't mentioned in the book, add your top ten **Things to Do** on the pages provided at the back.

Helpful Tips

The tips on the opposite page offer some guidelines to completing the **Things to Do**.

101 Things to Do Before You're Old and Boring

Tips

 Perform as many **Things to Do** as possible before it's too late and you're old and boring.

 Always carry this book with you (a **Thing to Do** may present itself at an unexpected moment).

 Some of the **Things to Do** in this book cannot be accomplished without a little courage.

 Be creative. It may take a bit of ingenuity to complete some of the **Things to Do**.

 You don't have to go it alone. Many of the **Things to Do** need or will simply be more fun with the help of your friends.

 Be quick. Fill out the form as soon as you've completed a **Thing to Do,** before you forget the details.

 If at first you don't succeed, keep trying. Some **Things to Do** may take a few attempts to complete and lots of practice.

 Push yourself. Do things you would normally avoid doing.

Above all, have fun. The **Things to Do** are ways to enhance your daily life.

101 Things to Do Before You're Old and Boring

Some Things You Will Need

Here is a list of some of the items you will need to complete the **101 Things to Do Before You're Old and Boring**. You don't need to have them all before you start, but it's advisable to at least have a pen, a pair of scissors, glue, a camera, access to a computer, and some money. You can get hold of the other items as you continue through the list, but the willingness to learn, a sense of adventure, spontaneity, a mischievous spirit, a sense of humor, a good imagination, and optimism are all up to you.

- ☐ A secret hiding place for this book!
- ☐ A pen
- ☐ A pair of scissors
- ☐ Glue
- ☐ A camera
- ☐ A computer
- ☐ Some money
- ☐ A photocopier
- ☐ Understanding parents
- ☐ Foulmouthed parents
- ☐ A little help from strangers
- ☐ Lots of help from your friends
- ☐ An overactive imagination
- ☐ A reckless spirit
- ☐ A sense of adventure
- ☐ A talent for something unusual
- ☐ Spontaneity
- ☐ Optimism
- ☐ A helpful streak
- ☐ A mischievous streak
- ☐ A head for heights
- ☐ A strong stomach
- ☐ A need for speed
- ☐ Basic cooking skills
- ☐ Luck
- ☐ Patience
- ☐ A haunted house
- ☐ A crowded elevator
- ☐ A bottle
- ☐ A message
- ☐ A musical instrument
- ☐ Any celebrity
- ☐ Various animals
- ☐ A tree
- ☐ A family tree
- ☐ A Christmas tree
- ☐ A passport
- ☐ A pack of cards
- ☐ A computer game
- ☐ A television
- ☐ A bike and/or skateboard
- ☐ A VCR/DVD player
- ☐ A cell phone
- ☐ A mountain
- ☐ Fruit
- ☐ Vegetables
- ☐ Advance planning
- ☐ A good/bad singing voice
- ☐ Junk
- ☐ A stone
- ☐ Hair dye
- ☐ Wakefulness
- ☐ Sleepiness
- ☐ Patience
- ☐ A swimming pool
- ☐ Snow
- ☐ Sand
- ☐ A tent
- ☐ A secret language
- ☐ A sense of humor

101 Things to Do Before You're Old and Boring

Important Information

WARNING:

WHEN EMBARKING ON THE *101 THINGS TO DO BEFORE YOU'RE OLD AND BORING*, PLEASE PROCEED WITH CARE.

FOR SOME OF THE *THINGS TO DO* YOU WILL NEED THE SUPERVISION OF AN ADULT. IF IN DOUBT, CONSULT AN ADULT ANYWAY.

THE AUTHORS AND PUBLISHER ACCEPT NO RESPONSIBILITY FOR ANY ACCIDENTS THAT OCCUR AS A RESULT OF USING THIS BOOK.

101 Things to Do Before You're Old and Boring

The List

1. ☐ Send a Message in a Bottle
2. ☐ Run up an Escalator the Wrong Way
3. ☐ Make an Origami Crane
4. ☐ Learn How to Tell When Someone Likes You (and When They Don't)
5. ☐ Keep a Dream Diary
6. ☐ Touch These Creatures
7. ☐ Prepare Yourself for Fame
8. ☐ Learn to Play an Instrument
9. ☐ Play a Computer Game to the End
10. ☐ Have an Embarrassing Moment and Get Over It
11. ☐ Get Your School Involved in a World Record Attempt
12. ☐ Paint a Picture Good Enough to Hang on the Wall
13. ☐ Learn to Whistle (and Make Other Noises)
14. ☐ See a Ghost
15. ☐ Fart and Burp
16. ☐ Make a Swear Box
17. ☐ Act in a Play
18. ☐ Win Something
19. ☐ Make a T-shirt
20. ☐ Stay Up All Night
21. ☐ Sleep All Day
22. ☐ Invent a Secret Code
23. ☐ Learn to Do a Card Trick
24. ☐ Grow Something from a Seed
25. ☐ Start a Collection
26. ☐ Help Save the Planet
27. ☐ Turn Back Time
28. ☐ Learn to Do a Party Trick
29. ☐ Climb to the Top of a Mountain
30. ☐ Make a One-Minute Movie
31. ☐ Host a Party
32. ☐ Visit . . .
33. ☐ Learn to Bake a Cake
34. ☐ Hide a Treasure and Leave a Map for Friends to Find
35. ☐ Learn How to Ask Someone Out (and How to Dump Them)
36. ☐ Start Your Own Blog
37. ☐ Write Lyrics for a Song
38. ☐ Make a Time Capsule
39. ☐ Be a Genius
40. ☐ Take Care of an Animal
41. ☐ Learn to Like These Foods
42. ☐ April Fool Someone
43. ☐ Do Something Charitable
44. ☐ Teach Your Grandparents Something New
45. ☐ Invent a New Game
46. ☐ Go as Fast as You Can
47. ☐ Make Your Own Buttons
48. ☐ Watch These Films
49. ☐ Read These Books
50. ☐ Pretend to Be Ill Convincingly
51. ☐ Save Your Allowance for a Month and Spend It All at Once
52. ☐ Learn to Swim
53. ☐ Succeed at Something You're Bad At
54. ☐ Be a Daredevil
55. ☐ Invent a New Trend

101 Things to Do Before You're Old and Boring

The List

Send a Message in a Bottle

Throwing a bottle with a message in it out to sea is traditionally a form of SOS. But it can also be an exciting way to make contact with people who live far away. Only the forces of nature and chance can help your message reach someone. Be patient. It could be years before it's found!

Bottling It Up

- Start your message with something like, "Congratulations on finding this message in a bottle. Please send an e-mail stating who you are and where you found the bottle." Then introduce yourself, including your name, the country you live in, and your e-mail address. Don't forget to date it! Write your message in as many different languages as you can.
- Put a present in the bottle for the person who finds it. It could be something useful—like matches or a whistle, in case your bottle reaches someone on a desert island—or something that you feel represents you or where you come from. Include a request that the person who finds it reseals the bottle and throws it back into the sea for someone else to find.
- Alternatively, start your message with something like, "Help! I'm stranded on a desert island," and write a little story about how you got there, how long you've been there, and how you're managing to survive. The trouble with this is that you'll never know if your bottle was ever found.
- Seal your bottle well. You don't want the message to get ruined.
- If you can't get to the ocean, you can always drop your bottle in a river.

Cosmic "message in a bottle": In 1977 the Voyager spacecraft flew a golden disk containing images, words, and sounds chosen to represent life on earth into space. The spacecraft passed out of our solar system in 2003. There has been no response yet!

Send a Message in a Bottle **Form**

Once you have completed this **Thing to Do**,
stick your Achieved Star here and fill in the form

Achieved

Date you sent your message

| m | m | d | d | y | y | y | y |

Where were you when you threw
your bottle into the ocean/river?

Date you received a reply

| m | m | d | d | y | y | y | y |

How long did it take for a reply?

| y | y | | m | m | | d | d |

Which country did your
message reach?

How many miles did it travel?

| 0 | 0 | 0 | 0 | 0 | 0 |

Who found it?

What did your message say? Write it below

Color in the
countries on the
map where you
threw your message
in a bottle into the
ocean and where it
ended up

At the same time, you could complete these **Things to Do**
52: Learn to Swim • 67: Build the Ultimate Sand Castle and Have Fun in the Sun
76: Learn to Say Useful Phrases in Other Languages

Run up an Escalator the Wrong Way

You need plenty of stamina for this. When you're standing at the bottom of an escalator, running up it doesn't seem such a daunting prospect. After all, they move pretty slowly, and you can easily see the top. However, you've got to remember that an average escalator is one and a half times longer than a staircase of the same size. And don't forget that the steps are much higher and will require more exertion. Still up for the challenge?

Running to Stand Still

- Find an escalator. Shopping malls are probably your best bet, or if you live near a subway, you've got plenty of choice.
  Start with a short one and pace yourself, or you'll run out of steam before you reach the top. It's a long, humiliating way down if you fail.
- Make sure you've got appropriate footwear on and you're not wearing any clothes that might trip you up or get caught in the escalator.
- Use an empty escalator. Other users won't be too happy if you barge past them and you might get told off. They'll also block your way and slow you down.
- If you want a real challenge, try escalators at major hubs on the New York city MTA. The F stop at Roosevelt Island has some of the longest escalators in the MTA system.
- Remember, where there is an up escalator, there is a down one too!

World record–breaking escalators: The longest series of escalators—Central-Mid-Levels, Hong Kong (2,625 ft.); the shortest—Okadaya More's Shopping Mall, Kawasaki-shi, Japan (33 in.); the longest in the United States—Wheaton Station, Washington, D.C. (508 ft.)

Run up an Escalator the Wrong Way Form

Once you have completed this **Thing to Do**,
stick your Achieved Star here and fill in the form

Achieved

Date of your escalator run

| m | m | d | d | y | y | y | y |

Where was the escalator?

Running up the down

Did you make it all the way to the top? [y/n] If no, mark on the diagram how far up the escalator you got

How many steps did the escalator have? [0 0]

How fast did you run up it (in seconds)? [0 0]

How many attempts did it take? [0 0]

Were there any people on the escalator? [y/n]

If yes, did they block your way? [y/n]

Did you race against your friends? [y/n]

Date of your escalator run

| m | m | d | d | y | y | y | y |

Where was the escalator?

Running down the up

Did you make it to the bottom? [y/n] If no, mark on the diagram how far down the escalator you got

How many steps did the escalator have? [0 0]

How fast did you run down it (in seconds)? [0 0]

How many attempts did it take? [0 0]

Were there any people on the escalator? [y/n]

If yes, did they block your way? [y/n]

Did you race against your friends? [y/n]

At the same time, you could complete these **Things to Do**
46: Go as Fast as You Can
69: Make a Scene in a Public Place

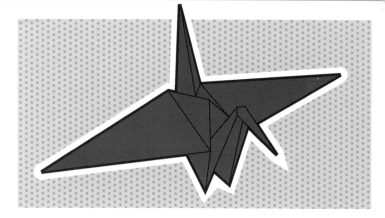

Make an Origami Crane

Origami is the art of folding paper to create intricate designs. Its history is vague, but historians believe the roots of origami began in China with the invention of paper back in the second century. Introduced into Japan in the sixth century, origami gradually, over many centuries, became a highly developed art form and a popular pastime.

Only the simplest origami designs survived through history, but the crane is the most famous of them and one of the first to have been written down. There is a Japanese legend that if you make one thousand origami cranes, your dreams will come true. So make a wish and get folding!

In the Fold

- You can make pretty much anything out of paper using origami, from dragons to dinosaurs, birds to boats, aliens to airplanes. But be warned! Some are simple to make; others are incredibly hard. Master the crane before moving on to other designs.
- Did you know that the maximum number of times you can fold an $8^{1}/_{2} \times 11$ inch piece of paper in half (halving the size of it with each fold) is seven times? Go on—try it!
- Next time you owe someone money, pay them back with an elephant! You can make origami creatures out of dollar bills too. Don't try this with your homework though. Your teacher won't be so impressed!

Origami rules! Many people believe that only one piece of square-shaped paper should be used. However, evidence shows that over the centuries people have used techniques such as cutting, pasting, using different shapes of paper, and more than one sheet!

Make an Origami Crane **Form**

Once you have completed this **Thing to Do**,
stick your Achieved Star here and fill in the form

Achieved

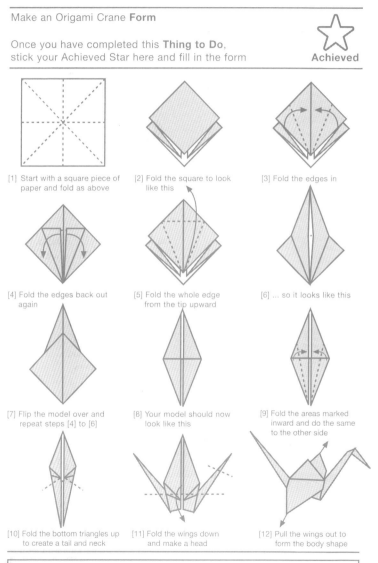

[1] Start with a square piece of paper and fold as above

[2] Fold the square to look like this

[3] Fold the edges in

[4] Fold the edges back out again

[5] Fold the whole edge from the tip upward

[6] ... so it looks like this

[7] Flip the model over and repeat steps [4] to [6]

[8] Your model should now look like this

[9] Fold the areas marked inward and do the same to the other side

[10] Fold the bottom triangles up to create a tail and neck

[11] Fold the wings down and make a head

[12] Pull the wings out to form the body shape

At the same time, you could complete these **Things to Do**
6: Touch These Creatures • 11: Get Your School Involved in a World Record
Attempt • 28: Learn to Do a Party Trick • 77: Make Your Own Greeting Cards

He loves me,
he loves me not...

Learn How to Tell When Someone Likes You (and When They Don't)

It's really hard to tell if someone likes you. One minute you're convinced that they do, but the next they're not even talking to you anymore. All those playing-hard-to-get games can really make your head hurt. If you're ever to get the courage to ask someone out, you need to know that there is at least some chance they'll say yes. Fortunately, there are a few subtle ways to tell if they like you. Learn some vital body-language tips here.

My Friend Likes You

- **Positive signs:** They sit or stand very close to you when possible • They playfully tease you a lot • They send you lots of text messages • They seem nervous around you • They gaze at you or look away when you make eye contact (the shy ones) • They seem to be in the same place as you A LOT • They laugh at your jokes, even the terrible ones • They show a lot of interest in your love life • They get **their** friend to tell you that they like you.
- **Unreliable signs:** They tease you a lot, sometimes nastily • They laugh at you a lot • They don't acknowledge your existence • They ask for help with their homework • They invite you to their party • They joke about the two of you going out with each other • **Your** friend tells you that this person likes you.
- Whatever you do, don't rely on love-prediction games, horoscopes, numerology, and so on. They're fun, but there's no evidence that they work!

More body-language signs: Do they look at your lips when you're talking? Do they find excuses to touch your hand, arm, or back? Do their movements echo yours? Watch their eyes—some scientists believe our pupils get bigger when we look at someone we like.

Learn How to Tell When Someone
Likes You (and When They Don't) **Form**
Once you have completed this **Thing to Do**,
stick your Achieved Star here and fill in the form

Achieved

Do they like me?

Take this quick quiz to find out if you're reading the signs correctly . . .

1. Do they tease you a lot?
a) Yes, we're always making friendly jibes at each other.
b) Sometimes—if I do or say something stupid.
c) Very often—and sometimes it makes me want to cry.

2. How often do you catch them gazing at you?
a) A lot, and if I catch their eye, they go red and look away quickly in embarrassment.
b) Sometimes our eyes meet, but they look lost in thought.
c) Occasionally. They're usually pointing and laughing too.

3. Do their pupils get bigger when they talk to you?
a) Yes, and I've also noticed they seem to glance at my lips a lot when I'm talking.
b) Sometimes—especially if it's a bit gloomy.
c) They never talk to me, so I wouldn't know.

4. How often do they send you text messages?
a) A lot, and often for no particular reason or just to ask me what I'm up to and who I'm with.
b) Quite often. It depends how much I text them.
c) Never. But that's because they don't have my number.

5. Do they seem to find excuses to sit or stand next to you?
a) Yes, they're always asking to borrow stuff or making excuses to talk to me about something.
b) From time to time—especially if they need help with something.
c) No. They say I smell.

6. Does anyone else think this person likes you?
a) Yes, their best friend told me they do.
b) A mutual friend thought we were really well suited and that we'd definitely get together eventually.
c) Yes, my best friend thinks I have a great chance.

7. Have they ever asked you out?
a) Yes, they've asked me if I want to go for coffee.
b) They asked me to their birthday party, but there were a lot of other people invited too.
c) Not really—although they did once ask me to "Go and take a running jump."

8. How do they behave when you're alone together?
a) Nervous. They seem to play with their hair or ear quite a lot and laugh at all my stupid jokes.
b) They're fairly relaxed and normal.
c) They ignore me.

Now add up your scores: a = 3, b = 2, c = 1

19–24: The signs are great. What are you waiting for? Make a move before they move on!

13–18: It sounds like they probably like you—the question is how much. You could take a risk and just go for it, or take time to do a bit more research. As a final test, you could try talking about someone else (real or imaginary) you like in front of them and see how they react. Jealousy is easy to spot.

8–11: Oh, dear. Time to set your sights on someone else, or you risk making a complete fool of yourself.

At the same time, you could complete these **Things to Do**
35: **Learn How to Ask Someone Out (and How to Dump Them)**
91: **Send a Valentine Card**

Keep a Dream Diary

Have you ever dreamed about being chased or failing a test you already took? Perhaps you've had mornings when you thought you'd got ready for school but realized you had just dreamed it? A dream diary allows you to capture those dreams before they're lost forever, and looking back on them might help you to make some sense out of them. Dreams can tell you a lot about what makes you happy, what you're worried or excited about, and many other things you never realized you were feeling.

Dream On

- Keep your diary and a pen by your bed. The memory of a dream can vanish into thin air very fast, so write it down as soon as you wake up.
- Some dreams have well-known meanings; e.g., flying can mean you feel in control of things, whereas falling might suggest you're anxious or insecure. You'll find information on the Internet that will help you interpret your dreams. Or you can buy a book about it.
- Ever had *déjà vu* (the feeling that you've done something before)? Well, although not much is known about it, one theory is that it may be linked to experiences you've had in forgotten dreams. Give science a helping hand by using your dream diary to see if your *déjà vu* experiences can be linked to dreams.
- Make a note if you keep having the same dream. Recurring dreams (often nightmares) are believed to be signs of a hidden stress in your life or a traumatic experience that has been buried in the memory.

Check out www.dreammoods.com for lots of help on the meaning of dreams. You can submit your own dreams for interpretation too! You might discover that even your most boring dreams have deep meanings—or maybe some of them really are just nonsense!

Keep a Dream Diary **Form**

Once you have completed this **Thing to Do**,
stick your Achieved Star here and fill in the form

☆ **Achieved**

Do you dream every night? `y/n`

How many of those dreams do you remember? `0 , 0`

Do you sleep-walk? `y/n`

Where is the farthest you've ever sleep-walked?

Have you ever talked in your sleep? `y/n`

If yes, what did you say?

Have you ever dreamed about someone famous? `y/n`

If yes, who was it?

Have you ever had a premonition? `y/n`

If yes, what did your dream predict?

Have you ever dreamed about ...

Running and getting nowhere?

Flying?

Falling?

Being late for school or an exam?

Going to school in your underwear?

Getting up and going out?

What's the scariest dream you've ever had?

What's the best dream you've ever had?

At the same time, you could complete these **Things to Do**
20: Stay Up All Night • 21: Sleep All Day
36: Start Your Own Blog • 38: Make a Time Capsule

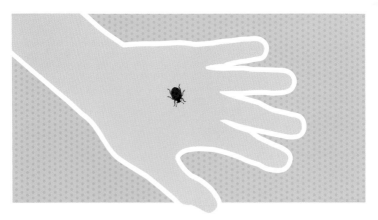

Touch These Creatures

There are millions of different creatures on earth, from aardvarks to zebras, from fleas to whales. Some you'll never get to touch, and in the case of the huge and vicious or the small and poisonous ones, that's just as well. But for creatures you're almost certain to come across, wouldn't it be better to get over any irrational fears now than be a scared and phobic adult? The longer you leave it, the harder it will be.

Animal Antics

- You only have to mention the word *spider* to some people and they'll be standing on a chair screaming. But remember, just because it's ugly, covered in hair, has eight eyes and as many legs, and can run like the wind, doesn't mean it's going to hurt you.
- One day you might find one of these creatures in your house or injured outside. Make sure you are the one who rescues in this situation, not the one who needs rescuing!
- Be gentle! Some of these creatures are fragile, so be careful not to hurt or squeeze them. Some can also give a nasty bite. Where possible, touch the domestic, not the wild, variety.

Other Animals
You've Touched

Animal name here

Animal name here

Animal name here

Animal name here

Animal name here

Animal name here

Common phobias: Zoophobia (animals), insectophobia (insects), arachnophobia (spiders), ichthyophobia (fish), ornithophobia (birds). Do you think some ichthyophobes could be hydrophobic (water) or ornithophobes, aviophobic (flying)?

Touch These Creatures **Form**

Once you have completed this **Thing to Do**,
stick your Achieved Star here and fill in the form

Achieved

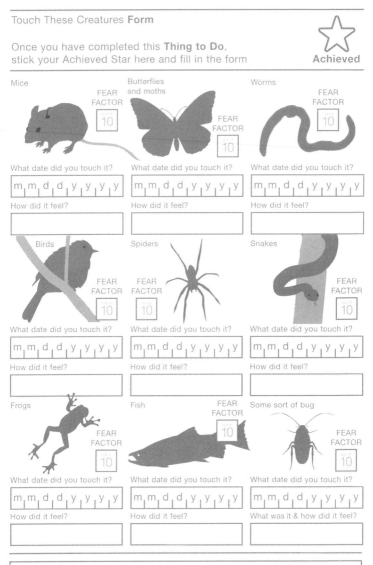

Mice

FEAR FACTOR
10

What date did you touch it?

m m d d y y y y

How did it feel?

Butterflies and moths

FEAR FACTOR
10

What date did you touch it?

m m d d y y y y

How did it feel?

Worms

FEAR FACTOR
10

What date did you touch it?

m m d d y y y y

How did it feel?

Birds

FEAR FACTOR
10

What date did you touch it?

m m d d y y y y

How did it feel?

Spiders

FEAR FACTOR
10

What date did you touch it?

m m d d y y y y

How did it feel?

Snakes

FEAR FACTOR
10

What date did you touch it?

m m d d y y y y

How did it feel?

Frogs

FEAR FACTOR
10

What date did you touch it?

m m d d y y y y

How did it feel?

Fish

FEAR FACTOR
10

What date did you touch it?

m m d d y y y y

How did it feel?

Some sort of bug

FEAR FACTOR
10

What date did you touch it?

m m d d y y y y

What was it & how did it feel?

At the same time, you could complete these **Things to Do**
3: **Make an Origami Crane** • 32: **Visit...**
40: **Take Care of an Animal** • 75: **Watch a Tadpole Grow into a Frog**

Prepare Yourself for Fame

We've all tried to imagine what it would be like to be famous. Taken to the shops in a chauffeur-driven limo, being treated like royalty, and waited on hand and foot (if your parents spoil you a lot, this may already sound familiar!). These days, being a celebrity is a job in itself—it can happen to almost anyone, and some people are truly awful at it. So don't be negative about your ambitions to be rich and famous—just make sure that when you get there, you know how to behave and don't make a fool of yourself.

When Will I Be Famous?

- When you're walking down the red carpet at a film premiere and people are screaming at you for an autograph, you should have your signature practiced to perfection. Make it suitably flamboyant, and never refuse to give it to someone. Practice your superstar walk too.
- You'll need to be one step ahead fashion-wise. Turn heads without looking like you're in fancy clothes. Ask friends to take photos of you to help you discover your best angle, and get used to being in front of the camera. Practice smiling and keeping cool in tricky situations. You have to be on your best behavior as a celebrity, or the press will have you for dinner.
- Imagine your life as a celebrity and rehearse an interview. People will want to know everything about you, but it's up to you how much you give away. You don't want to seem stuck-up, but you also don't want to upset the people you care about by broadcasting your private life.

Brand yourself: Is your name glamorous and catchy enough for a life of fame? Lots of celebrities have (understandably) changed theirs. Ja Rule was born Jeffrey Atkins, Tom Cruise was Thomas Mapother IV, and Marilyn Monroe was Norma Jean Mortenson.

Prepare Yourself for Fame **Form**

Once you have completed this **Thing To Do**,
stick your Achieved Star here and fill in the form

Achieved

When do you predict you'll
become famous? | 2 _ _ _ |

Will you give yourself a stage name? | y/n |

If yes, what will it be?

How do you predict you'll achieve fame?

At what age will you become famous? | 0 0 |

What kind of home will you live in?

Where will it be?

How many servants will you have? | 0 0 |

Which celebrity will you marry?

How many children will you have? | 0 0 |

What type of car will you drive?

How much money do
you estimate you'll have? | $ |

THINGS TO DO

How many pets will you have? | 0 0 |

What will they be?

What stores will you shop at?

What age do you think you'll live to? | 0 0 |

Please may I have your autograph?

Once you have perfected your signature, sign your name here

Come back to this book in 20
years and fill in the section below

For future use

Did you become famous? | y/n |

If yes, was it for the
reason you stated above? | y/n |

Do you enjoy fame? | y/n |

Did you marry
someone famous? | y/n |

At the same time, you could complete these **Things to Do**
56: Know Who Your Friends Are • 100: Meet Someone Famous
101: Decide What You Want to Be When You Grow Up

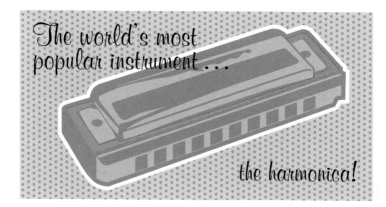

The world's most popular instrument...

the harmonica!

Learn to Play an Instrument

Have you ever found in school music lessons that you never get to play the instrument you want? Instead of getting to bang drums and crash cymbals, you end up with the tambourine—or worse still, cowbells. Of course, everyone can play at least one great instrument: the air guitar. It's easy to pick up and play right away, and no one can tell you you're terrible. But it's time to put down those bells and that air guitar and learn a serious instrument. How else will you get to play onstage with your favorite musicians in front of hundreds of fans?

Thank You for the Music

- There's a whole world of instruments out there to pluck, bow, hit, strum, or blow. Listen to different types of music to familiarize yourself with some of the less obvious ones. It's important that you love the sound of the instrument. Don't let others pressure you into learning something you don't want to.
- Maybe your parents are already forcing you to take music lessons, and you hate it. Until you get pretty good at your instrument, it might not be very rewarding. But it's worth persevering—because in the end, you'll be able to impress and entertain people with your musical talent. So hang in there and work hard at it. Practice makes perfect!
- As soon as you feel ready, join a music group or start a band because playing with other people is great fun and performing in front of people may be scary, but it's exciting too.

 Annoy your parents by playing your instrument loudly while they're trying to watch TV. If they shout at you, just tell them how important it is for you to practice. They can't argue with that.

Learn to Play an Instrument **Form**

Once you have completed this **Thing to Do**,
stick your Achieved Star here and fill in the form   **Achieved**

Choose your instrument from the following categories:

= Coolness rating (1–10)

Percussion   Strings   Keyboards   Brass   Woodwind

Which category did you choose?

Which instrument did you choose?

What style of music do you like?

What was the first piece of music you learned?

Can you play in that style?   y/n

Have you played in
front of anyone else yet?   y/n

If yes, who, and how did it go?

How many hours do you practice
a week?   0,0

Date and time of your first lesson

m,m,d,d,y,y,y,y   :

How well do you rate your instrument playing?

☆ ☆ ☆ ☆ ☆
Poor   OK   Good   Very good   Excellent

Did you choose to learn your instrument
because you wanted to?   y/n

How do your parents rate your instrument playing?

☆ ☆ ☆ ☆ ☆
Poor   OK   Good   Very good   Excellent

If no, who forced it upon you?

At the same time, you could complete these **Things to Do**
7: **Prepare Yourself for Fame** • 58: **Start a Band**
72: **See Your Music Idol Perform Live** • 86: **Sing in Front of an Audience**

Play a Computer Game to the End

It's too easy to get hooked on a computer game. They lull you into a false sense of security by allowing you to do reasonably well, and then ZAP!— some gruesome creature, hidden sniper, kung-fu fighter, or the Brazilian football team comes out of nowhere and suddenly it's GAME OVER. Before long, you've clocked up forty hours of playing and you're still nowhere near completing it. It's all you can think about, all you can see when you close your eyes. Nothing is more important than finishing this game!

Take It to the Next Level

- Complete the game without help. Your sense of achievement will be far greater if you do it on your own. Don't be a cheat if you can help it!*
- Depending on the game, you may be able to save your position. Use this wisely, saving only when your energy is high and you're just about to face a difficult bit. Then save again if you manage to get past that bit and have enough energy to continue.
- To keep your stamina and concentration up, take regular breaks. Get up to stretch or walk around every 20 minutes, as it reduces the risk of RSI (repetitive strain injury) or DVT (deep vein thrombosis). RSI affects hand, arm, or shoulder muscles, causing great pain if they are overused—especially if they're repeating the same movement over and over (like hitting the FIRE button!). DVT is a condition people can get on very long flights, where big periods of inactivity can lead to blood clots. Don't become a victim! Use that PAUSE or SAVE button!

---

*At your wits' end? If you do get completely stuck and desperately need help, turn to the Internet. There are plenty of sites dedicated to guiding you through your impossible computer game. You'll kick yourself when you find out how to finish it though!

Play a Computer Game to the End **Form**

Once you have completed this **Thing to Do**,
stick your Achieved Star here and fill in the form

Achieved

What game have you been playing?

Date and time you completed the game

m m d d y y y y   :

Date and time you started the game

m m d d y y y y   :

How long have you been playing the game in total?

0 0 Months   0 0 Weeks   0 0 Days   0 0 Hours

Write your high score in here

0 0 0 0 0 0 0 0

What type of game was it?

Adventure   Arcade   War/combat   Card and board game   Sport/racing   Other

☐ ☐ ☐ ☐ ☐ ☐

If other, please specify

Why did you cheat?

How did you cheat?

How many levels did the game have?   0 0

Could you choose what level of difficulty to play the game at?   y/n

If yes, what level did you choose?

Was it hard to stop playing?   y/n

Did you get told off for playing it too much?   y/n

Are you the best person at this game that you know?   y/n

If no, who is?

How hard was the game overall?

☆ ☆ ☆ ☆ ☆
Easy   Quite easy   Hard   Very hard   Impossible

How would you rate the game?

☆ ☆ ☆ ☆ ☆
Poor   OK   Good   Very good   Excellent

Was the game too hard to finish?   y/n   Did you cheat?   y/n

At the same time, you could complete these **Things to Do**
20: Stay Up All Night • 45: Invent a New Game
53: Succeed at Something You're Bad At • 61: Join a Club

Have an Embarrassing Moment and Get Over It

There are things in life that you just have to accept, and being totally humiliated is one of them. Sure, some embarrassing moments could be avoided. But we're all human and we all make mistakes, so the best thing to do is take it on the chin and laugh at yourself before someone else does. This is a great way to defuse the situation. You can't go back in time and change things, so either laugh and forget it or learn from it and move on.

Embarrassing situations come in all forms. They include: farting loudly, saying something stupid, being sick, wetting yourself, or falling over or walking into something in public; being caught getting changed, sitting on the toilet, going out with your fly undone or skirt tucked into your underwear, or singing or talking to yourself; forgetting the lines in a play or speech, or messing up in a music performance; and asking someone out only for them to say no. Ouch!

Always Look on the Bright Side of Life

- Remember, it could always be worse. You could be caught with no clothes on, locked outside your house on the busiest road in town while your street is being broadcast live on the national news.
- Write down your embarrassing moment on the form. By writing it down, you'll help to banish your demons and get it out of your system. You'll also have a great story to tell people when you're older and over it (and you'll probably have had worse happen to you anyway!).

Ever goofed up without anybody noticing?—Until you made a big deal of it, that is! Blushing, making faces, or stopping what you're doing are bound to get you noticed and cause more embarrassment. With small goof-ups, try pretending nothing happened.

Have an Embarrassing Moment and Get Over It **Form**

Once you have completed this **Thing to Do**,
stick your Achieved Star here and fill in the form

Achieved

What happened was...

When did this moment happen?

| m | m | d | d | y | y | y | y |

How embarrassing would you rate the incident?

Not that bad   Quite   Very   Extremely   I can't talk about it

Do people still remind you of it? y/n

In hindsight, was it really that bad? y/n

Are you over it? y/n

Can you laugh about it now? y/n

At the same time, you could complete these **Things to Do**
15: Fart and Burp • 35: Learn How to Ask Someone Out (and How to Dump Them) • 54: Be a Daredevil • 88: Blame Someone Else

Get Your School Involved in a World Record Attempt

For this **Thing to Do**, your strength lies in your numbers. Think along the lines of the most people doing an activity at the same time, like brushing teeth (mind you, if you attempt this one, you'll have to beat the record of 10,240 people, held by Chinese students). Or you could try to break a record in making something—many hands make light work. In 2004 Eisenhower Junior High School in Utah broke the record for the longest paper clip chain (it used 1,560,377 paper clips and measured over 22 miles!). Or if your numbers will allow you to take turns and work in shifts, you could try to do an activity for a long period of time, like a sports marathon where you attempt the longest game of something. You don't have to go after an existing record, of course. Make up a brand-new one!

Simply the Best

- Decide on your world record attempt, and suggest the idea to your teachers. Make it something fun so that even if you don't break the record, you've had a good time anyway.
- You'll need to make an application to Guinness World Records (www.guinnessworldrecords.com) if you want your achievement to be officially recognized, and fill out a form. There may be guidelines you have to follow if you're going to try to break an existing record.
- The more people involved, the merrier. Don't stop at your school— get your friends' families and other local schools involved as well.

How big is your school? Founded in 1959, the pupils at City Montessori School in Lucknow, India, didn't have to do much to break a world record except attend school. By 2002 there were over 26,000 pupils, making it the largest school in the world.

Get Your School Involved in
a World Record Attempt **Form**
Once you have completed this **Thing to Do**,
stick your Achieved Star here and fill in the form

Achieved

This is to certify that...

Your name here

attempted a world record for...

The record you attempted here

The attempt was a total...

Success! / Failure!*

*Delete as applicable

Record attempt details

Date you attempted the record?

| m | m | d | d | y | y | y | y |

Where did the attempt take place?

How many people were involved?

| 0 | 0 | 0 | 0 | 0 | 0 | 0 | 0 |

Was it difficult to attempt? y/n

How long did the attempt take?

| 0 | 0 | Months | 0 | 0 | Weeks | 0 | 0 | Days |

How would you rate your performance?

☆1 ☆2 ☆3 ☆4 ☆5

Did you get an entry in the
Guinness World Records book? y/n

At the same time, you could complete these **Things to Do**
3: **Make an Origami Crane** • 25: **Start a Collection** • 46: **Go as Fast as You Can**
52: **Learn to Swim** • 82: **Learn to Skip Stones** • 98: **Drive Something**

Paint a Picture Good Enough to Hang on the Wall

Brighten up your house with an original work of art painted by you. Your painting doesn't have to be technically brilliant—lots of gifted artists produce paintings that look nothing like what they see in real life!

Impress and Express

- What would you like to paint? If you're stuck for ideas, how about a portrait? If you can't find anyone to sit still for hours while you paint, use a photograph. Or perhaps you have great views from your house. If so, why not paint the landscape? And if not, paint the view you'd like to see from your window.
- Have fun with it, and use your imagination to make the painting unique and original. Don't try to please others before you please yourself. Painting gives you the chance to express YOURSELF!
- Make sure you sign it and hang it in a prominent place so it's the first thing visitors see when they come into the house.
- Remember that the rest of your family have to live with your creation too; so if you want it to go up on the wall, don't make it offensive to anybody, or too offensive to the eye! All art is a matter of taste. If the rest of your family really doesn't like your masterpiece and you do, try not to be upset. Many of the world's greatest artists weren't appreciated in their own time, so this may be a good sign. Hang it in your bedroom. Either that, or give it to someone who will love it and hang it up no matter what, like your grandma.

 You don't have to stick with paint. Try using other media as well as, or instead of, paint. Try pens, pencils, colored pencils, ink, collage, paper, glue or pastels— whatever you like. Some artists have been known to use elephant dung!

Paint a Picture Good Enough
to Hang on the Wall **Form**
Once you have completed this **Thing to Do**,
stick your Achieved Star here and fill in the form

Achieved

Place a photograph of
your masterpiece here, or
redraw it and glue it here

Write the title of your masterpiece here

Did everyone like
your picture? | y/n | If no, who
didn't like it? | | Did it go on the
wall anyway? | y/n

At the same time, you could complete these **Things to Do**
53: Succeed At Something You're Bad At • **61: Join a Club**
78: Hold a Jumble Sale • **97: Learn to Take Great Photos**

Learn to Whistle (and Make Other Noises)

Whistling is a handy skill to have, perfect for grabbing someone's attention, showing your appreciation, or keeping yourself company with a little tune. But not everyone can do it. Practicing on your own is the best way to learn, but don't worry if it doesn't happen right away—practice makes perfect.

The Art of Noise

- Whistle: Moisten your lips, then put the tip of your tongue against your bottom teeth. Now make an *o* with your lips and blow gently, trying to keep your tongue relaxed.
- Whistle with fingers (much louder): Place a finger from each hand (or two from the same hand) into your mouth. Curl your tongue up (as if you were about to say "la") so your fingers are touching the underside of your tongue, and blow gently, keeping the tongue relaxed.
- Pop: This is the easiest one. Put your index finger in your mouth and pull it out, dragging it across the inside of your cheek on the way.
- Water droplet: This is a hard sound to reproduce. Flick the outside of your cheek with your fingers, and at the same time move your mouth like a fish, so you are pushing air out of your cheeks.
- Animal noise: Choose an animal you'd like to imitate. Listen carefully to them and try to mimic the noise. A good way to alter the sound is by placing your hands over your mouth to muffle or amplify (cupping your hands).

Beatboxing (using the voice to imitate a drum machine) is hard, but if you can learn to do it like the professionals, you'll be a hit at parties. Alternatively, invent some sounds of your own (perhaps incorporate an animal noise or two) and create a unique beatbox.

Learn to Whistle (and Make Other Noises) **Form**

Once you have completed this **Thing to Do**,
stick your Achieved Star here and fill in the form

☆ Achieved

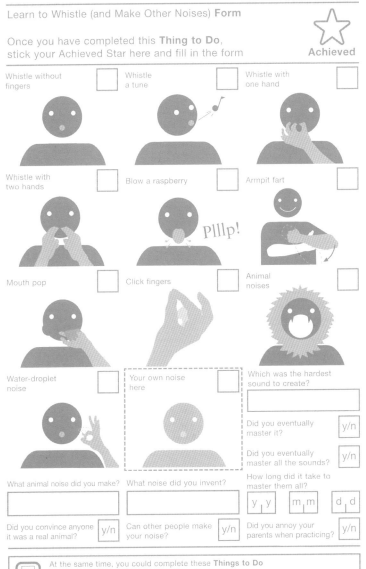

Whistle without fingers ☐

Whistle a tune ☐

Whistle with one hand ☐

Whistle with two hands ☐

Blow a raspberry ☐   Plllp!

Armpit fart ☐

Mouth pop ☐

Click fingers ☐

Animal noises ☐

Water-droplet noise ☐

Your own noise here ☐

Which was the hardest sound to create?

Did you eventually master it? y/n

Did you eventually master all the sounds? y/n

What animal noise did you make?

What noise did you invent?

How long did it take to master them all?
y y   m m   d d

Did you convince anyone it was a real animal? y/n

Can other people make your noise? y/n

Did you annoy your parents when practicing? y/n

At the same time, you could complete these **Things to Do**
15: Fart and Burp • 28: Learn to Do a Party Trick
69: Make a Scene in a Public Place • 72: See Your Music Idol Perform Live

See a Ghost

A ghost won't come to you; you've got to go in search of it. There are lots of places around the U.S. with paranormal activity. Just be sure that when you visit, you've got the essential pieces of ghost-hunting equipment.

Ghostbusting

- Cameras can show things the naked eye can't see. In many cases people have taken photos without being aware of any paranormal activity, but when the film was developed, figures appeared in the pictures that couldn't be seen at the time. So when you're in a haunted house, remember to take lots of photos. You might just catch a ghost.
- An audiocassette is the best way to capture EVP (electronic voice phenomena). So dig out that old Walkman (you can use the headphones as a microphone by plugging them into the MIC socket). You might not hear anything at the time, but like the camera phenomenon, on playback you may hear unexplained sounds and voices.

Haunted Places

Alamo (San Antonio, Texas)

Alcatraz (San Francisco Bay, California)

Battlefields of Gettysburg (Gettysburg, Pennsylvania)

Bell Witch Cave (Adams, Tennessee)

Boston Athenaeum (Boston, Massachusetts)

Central Park (New York, New York)

Cherry Hill Mansion (Albany, New York)

Devil's Tramping Ground (Salisbury, North Carolina)

Ford Theatre (Washington, D.C.)

Lincoln's Bedroom (White House, Washington, D.C.)

Lizzie Borden Bed & Breakfast Inn (Fall River, Massachusetts)

The Queen Mary (Long Beach, California)

Rathbone House (Lafayette Square, Washington, D.C.)

Three Sisters Rock (Georgetown, Washington, D.C.)

Winchester Mystery House (San Jose, California)

I ain't afraid of no ghost: Horror films and books would have us believe that ghosts are evil, but there is very little evidence of anyone having been hurt by one. A mischievous spirit may try to scare you, but don't let your fear conquer you. Ghosts are harmless…usually.

See a Ghost **Form**

Once you have completed this **Thing to Do**,
stick your Achieved Star here and fill in the form

☆ Achieved

What was the date and time of your sighting?

| m | m | d | d | y | y | y | y | | : |

Where were you when you saw it?

What did it look like?

Headless | Floating | A poltergeist (invisible) | Someone you knew | An animal | Other

If other, please specify

If you recognized the ghost, who was it?

What did you hear?

Laughing | Moaning | Clanking of chains | Talking or whispering | Screaming | Other

If other, please specify

How scared were you?

It didn't scare me | A little nervous | Shocked | Scared | Very scared | Petrified

Did you hunt for the ghost or was it luck?

Hunted for the ghost | Just lucky | Just unlucky

If you hunted, how many attempts did it take to see something? | 0 , 0

What did you feel?

Cold | Creepy | Like someone was watching you | Something touching you | Your hair standing on end | Other

If other, please specify

Did you capture it on camera?

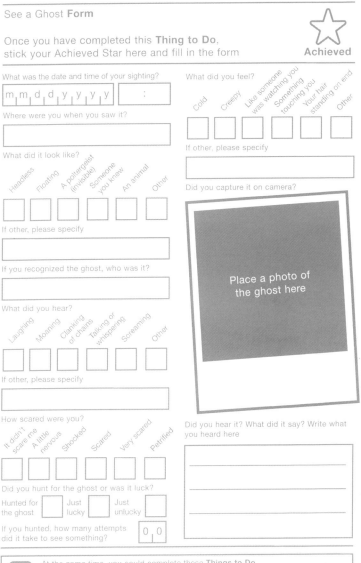
Place a photo of the ghost here

Did you hear it? What did it say? Write what you heard here

At the same time, you could complete these **Things to Do**
20: Stay Up All Night • 59: Camp Out in the Backyard
89: Learn to Stick Up for Yourself • 97: Learn to Take Great Photos

Fart and Burp

Everybody farts. If someone says they don't, then they're lying. Face facts: if you're alive, you fart.* On average, each person produces around a pint (or half a liter) of gas a day. That's about fourteen farts a day—and this includes girls! That's right. The "girls-don't-fart" excuse just isn't true. They fart just as much as boys, although they may make more of an effort to hide them.

And if that wasn't enough, we also burp about fifteen times a day. Yes, girls, you too. Farting and burping show us our bodies are doing a good job. They're as natural as the wind that blows, so they should be celebrated, not frowned upon.

Better Out Than In

- Fart in a confined space like a train. The best time is just as you're getting off, leaving the smell trapped inside but you safely outside. No one can escape until the next station. Try this trick in elevators too.
- Burp or fart loudly when it's quiet in a cinema, a theater, in assembly, at a wedding, or while you're kissing.
- Learn to make it look like somebody else did it. A good way is to look in their direction and raise your eyebrows at them. But remember the saying, "Those who smelt, it dealt it." Don't jump in to accuse someone else too quickly, or it will look suspicious. Soft targets for blame are your grandma or the dog.

---

*Let the dead R.I.P. Some of the gas in a fart is swallowed air, and some is produced by the bacteria that works in the gut to break down food. This bacteria continues to work even after a person has died, and occasionally the gas manages to escape as a fart!

Fart and Burp **Form**

Once you have completed this **Thing to Do**,
stick your Achieved Star here and fill in the form

★ Achieved

At the same time, you could complete these **Things to Do**
**10: Have an Embarrassing Moment and Get Over It • 13: Learn to Whistle
(and Make Other Noises) • 69: Make a Scene in a Public Place**

Make a Swear Box

This is one surefire way to make money…and fast! Your foulmouthed parents need to be taught a lesson for teaching you bad words. OK, so you've probably heard them all before, but why should it be rude and unacceptable for you to curse and not them? The best way to teach them this valuable lesson in how to talk nicely and not be a hypocrite is to hit them where it hurts—in their wallets!

I Swear I'll Never Do It Again

- Log each swear word they've taught you, and adjust the cost of the fine according to the offensiveness of the word.
- The swear box isn't solely for your parents; it also applies to people visiting the house. For instance, if a neighbor comes over to complain about the "*!'*●*!ing music," make sure you fine him or her before turning your stereo down.
- Warning! Your parents may try to be devious and use the same penalty system on you. You could end up being fined for not tidying up or not making the bed. Try to get around this by arguing that in law, you can only be punished for the bad things you do, not the good things you don't do. If that doesn't wash, you'd better abide by their rules to make sure they have absolutely no excuse for taking back any of the money they earned for you.

A great idea! Instead of swearing, you could encourage your parents to revive some far less offensive slang terms from times gone by, like "Doggone," "Leaping lizards," "Gee whiz," "Jeepers Creepers," and "Shucks."

Make a Swear Box **Form**

Once you have completed this **Thing to Do**,
stick your Achieved Star here and fill in the form

☆ **Achieved**

Since the introduction
of the swear box...

Swear word	Price	Culprit(s)	has the frequency of this word decreased?	y/n

Swear word	Price	Culprit(s)	has the frequency of this word decreased?	y/n

Swear word	Price	Culprit(s)	has the frequency of this word decreased?	y/n

Swear word	Price	Culprit(s)	has the frequency of this word decreased?	y/n

Swear word	Price	Culprit(s)	has the frequency of this word decreased?	y/n

Swear word	Price	Culprit(s)	has the frequency of this word decreased?	y/n

Swear word	Price	Culprit(s)	has the frequency of this word decreased?	y/n

Swear word	Price	Culprit(s)	has the frequency of this word decreased?	y/n

Swear word	Price	Culprit(s)	has the frequency of this word decreased?	y/n

Swear word	Price	Culprit(s)	has the frequency of this word decreased?	y/n

Are your parents swearing less now? | y/n

If no, are you still making money off them? | y/n

Have you told them it's their fault when you swear? | y/n

Who else has contributed?

What was your swear box total after a month?

THINGS TO DO

$ _____

At the same time, you could complete these **Things to Do**
**43: Do Something Charitable • 51: Save Your Pocket Money for a Month and
Spend It All at Once • 96: Glue Coins to the Floor**

Act in a Play

Ever wanted to be someone else? Well, acting allows you to do just that! It's ideal for show-offs, giving them the chance to do well and be truly in the spotlight. But if you're shy, you should give it a go too. Performing in front of an audience is a great confidence builder. The trick is to lose yourself in the part, forgetting yourself as well as the audience out there.

Come Out to Play

- If you want to be in the school play, you'll probably have to audition to prove you can play the part. Try to read the play beforehand so you know about the character you'd like to be and can get into the role.
- To make yourself believable, try method acting. This means "living" as your character while you are preparing for your part. Even if you've been given a small role (e.g., part of a crowd, a tree, Pirate 3), invent a personality and live it out on and off the stage.*
- It's embarrassing, but it's not the end of the world if you make a mistake. It's happened to all the best actors. All you can do is to carry on as if nothing had happened. If you forget your lines, make them up!
- If you don't get the part you want, the alternative is to stage your own play. Then you can take any role you like—including director! Get your friends together and rehearse a play. If you want to keep it simple, it could just be a scene from your favorite film or book. Use the living room, the yard, or the attic as your theater, and beg, borrow, or buy clothes from a charity shop for costumes.

---

 *Steal the limelight: If you're unhappy that you've been given a small role, do something dramatic to show what a great actor you are; e.g., speak your lines louder than anyone else or give your character an unusual accent. Everyone will remember you for it.

Act in a Play **Form**

Once you have completed this **Thing to Do**,
stick your Achieved Star here and fill in the form

Achieved

Date of the play	Did you have any lines? y/n	Did everything go according to plan? y/n
m m d d y y y y	What were your favorite lines?	If no, what happened?

What was the title of the play?

Where was the play held?

Which part did you play?

Describe your character

Did you get any wrong? y/n   Was this your most embarrassing moment? y/n

Draw the characters, the costumes, and the backdrops for the play below, or place a photograph below instead

At the same time, you could complete these **Things to Do**
7: **Prepare Yourself for Fame** • 30: **Make a One-Minute Movie**
83: **Dye Your Hair** • 86: **Sing in Front of an Audience**

Win Something

To win is to come out on top, to be the best, better than all the rest.
There are loads of different kinds of competitions, awards, and races to be
won. Some may require skill, others luck. Either way, winning gives you a
great feeling!

The Winner Takes It All

- Win a race: Field day is a good time to win a race. Winning in front of
  the whole school is a great feeling, and victory will be even sweeter if (a)
  you're competing against your greatest rival, (b) a prize is involved, or (c)
  someone you like is watching you run. If you're not very athletic,
  participating in a charity run would do just as well.
- Win a competition: Enter as many as you can—school ones, sporting
  ones, ones in magazines and newspapers or on the radio and TV. You're
  bound to win something eventually. Enter ones that require a special talent
  (if you have that talent), like writing or art competitions, and if that doesn't
  work, enter those that any idiot might stand a chance of winning. They're
  much more of a lottery; but someone has to win, and it could be you.
- The bigger the competition or race, the better. You won't get much
  satisfaction or recognition by winning a game of Scrabble against your
  grandma; but if you become Jeopardy champion, the memory of
  your victory will live with you forever. After winning a local
  competition, aim for a national or even an international one!

Young winners: The youngest person to ever receive an Oscar was 10-year-old Tatum
O'Neal. Her Oscar was for Best Supporting Actress in the film *Paper Moon* in 1973. The
youngest ever soccer World Cup winner was the Brazilian Pelé in 1958. He was just 17.

Win Something **Form**

Once you have completed this **Thing to Do**,
stick your Achieved Star here and fill in the form

☆ Achieved

Date you won something

m m d d y y y y

What did you win in?

How many competitors were there?

Where did you come in?

☐ First ☐ Second ☐ Third

Did you win through ... ☐ skill? ☐ luck?

If luck, how were you lucky?

What did you win?

[1] A rosette   [2] A trophy   [3] A medal   [4] A certificate   [5] A prize

[6] Money

[7] Tickets

[8] A meeting with a celebrity

If other, draw your prize here

[9] Other

What did the medal/trophy/rosette/certificate say on it?

If you won a prize, what was it?

If you won money, how much? $

If you won tickets, what were they for?

If you got to meet a celebrity, who was it?

At the same time, you could complete these **Things to Do**
46: Go as Fast as You Can
98: Drive Something

Make a T-shirt

Why buy a T-shirt with someone else's design on it when you could make your own? Get yourself a plain old white T-shirt and transform it using one of the techniques below.

Wear It with Pride

There are various ways to transfer your design onto a T-shirt.

- Method 1: Use tracing paper to trace your chosen design (e.g., the logo of your favorite band) with a pencil. Once you have the outline, turn the paper over and redraw over the lines. Then turn it over again, place the design into position on your T-shirt, and trace over it one last time. The design will appear lightly in pencil on the T-shirt. Using these pencil lines as a guide, you can then paint your design directly onto the T-shirt with fabric paints.
- Method 2: You could produce your own designs on a computer and then use the technique above, or print out your final design on special printer-friendly transfer paper and iron it straight onto a T-shirt.
- Method 3: Use a material called flock. This can be bought as iron-on letters (ideal if your design is just a few words), and it also comes by the yard if you want to cut out your own letters and shapes. You will have to use an iron to fix the flock in place on the T-shirt.

Silk screening involves making a stencil of your design, attaching it to a screen (usually made of silk), and squeezing ink through it onto the T-shirt. Warning: This method allows you to make lots of T-shirts, but the equipment is rather expensive.

Make a T-shirt **Form**

Once you have completed this **Thing to Do**,
stick your Achieved Star here and fill in the form

Achieved

Date you made the T-shirt

m m d d y y y y

Who was the T-shirt for?

How long did it take to do?

0 0 Days   0 0 Hours   0 0 Mins

Draw your T-shirt design below

Were you pleased
with the final result?   y/n

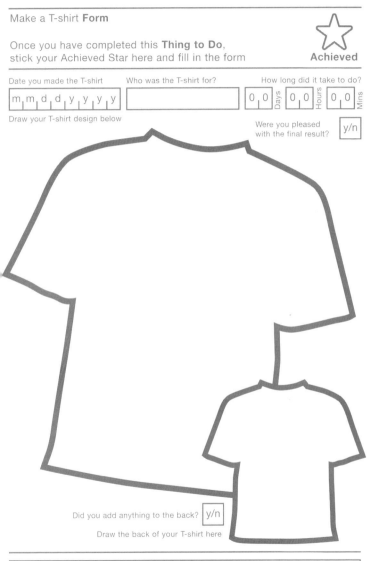

Did you add anything to the back?   y/n

Draw the back of your T-shirt here

At the same time, you could complete these **Things to Do**
25: Start a Collection • **47: Make Your Own Buttons**
55: Invent a New Trend

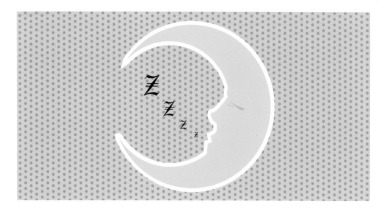

Stay Up All Night

Have you ever had a sleepover where you have your friends over for the night and have a pajama party? Well, this is the perfect excuse for another one, except this time no one is going to sleep over at all. Call it a "stayover" instead. Have your friends over, and do your best to keep each other awake all night with fun and games. Then the next morning, after you've watched the sunrise, send them home and move on to **Thing to Do** No. 21—spend a day catching up on lost sleep!

Join the Dawn Chorus

- This challenge will be too hard if you attempt it alone. Why? Because the ways you choose to entertain yourself on your own will probably involve doing things that make you drowsy, like watching films, reading, or playing computer games. Invite your friends over. Playing board games, party games, or just chatting are much more stimulating activities. And if one of you starts to fade, someone will be there to provide a friendly pinch!
- Don't eat loads of food—it'll make you feel sleepy. However, drinking coke or energy drinks should help to perk you up if you start fading. Throwing cold water on your face or getting some fresh air by sticking your head out of a window will help too. Don't sit in the same spot for too long—get up and move around. You need to be active to stop those eyelids from drooping.

 Get sponsored to stay awake for the whole night to help a charity. Your parents can't say no to that. The more friends involved, the more fun and money you'll get out of it. You could also raise money by taking bets on who falls asleep first.

Stay Up All Night Form

Once you have completed this **Thing to Do**,
stick your Achieved Star here and fill in the form

Achieved

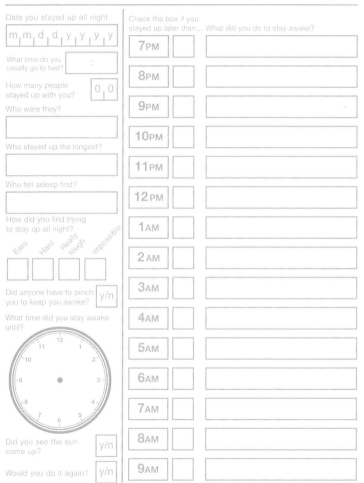

Date you stayed up all night

| m | m | d | d | y | y | y | y |

What time do you usually go to bed? | : |

How many people stayed up with you? | 0 | 0 |

Who were they?

Who stayed up the longest?

Who fell asleep first?

How did you find trying to stay up all night?

Easy   Hard   Really tough   Impossible

Did anyone have to pinch you to keep you awake? | y/n |

What time did you stay awake until?

Did you see the sun come up? | y/n |

Would you do it again? | y/n |

Check the box if you stayed up later than... What did you do to stay awake?

7PM	
8PM	
9PM	
10PM	
11PM	
12PM	
1AM	
2AM	
3AM	
4AM	
5AM	
6AM	
7AM	
8AM	
9AM	

At the same time, you could complete these **Things to Do**
9: Play a Computer Game to the End • 14: See a Ghost
21: Sleep All Day • 31: Host a Party • 48: Watch These Films

Sleep All Day

It can be SO hard to get out of bed sometimes. There are mornings when it just feels impossible, even though you know you've got to get up—in fact, especially when you know you have to! Well, maybe you should just stay in bed. It's a fact that one third of your life is spent sleeping. So how can anyone tell you to get out of bed when all you're doing is getting three nights worth of sleep in at one shot on the same day!

Sleep Easy

- The idea is to spend the day actually asleep, not just hanging out in your bedroom. Block out as much daylight as possible, pop in some earplugs, and remember to turn off your alarm clock. If you've just stayed up all night (**Thing to Do** No. 20), it'll be much easier.
- Your body clock won't be easily fooled by your efforts to simulate nighttime, and unless you're completely exhausted, staying asleep will be hard. Don't be tempted to get up though, even if you're wide-awake. Make sure you have a school textbook by your bed or a slow, dull movie to watch to give your mind and body the encouragement it needs to shut down again.
- Stock up on drinks, snacks (nothing with lots of sugar though, as this will wake you up), and sleep-inducing entertainment before you start. You should only need to leave your bed to go to the bathroom.
- If you get told off for being lazy, say you're doing brain work. It's true—parts of the brain are very much awake while you sleep.*

---

*REM: If you watch someone while they're asleep you may notice their eyes moving fast under the eyelids. This is called rapid eye movement, and it happens when the brain is very active and we're sleeping lightly. It's during periods of REM sleep that we dream.

Sleep All Day **Form**

Once you have completed this **Thing to Do**,
stick your Achieved Star here and fill in the form

Achieved

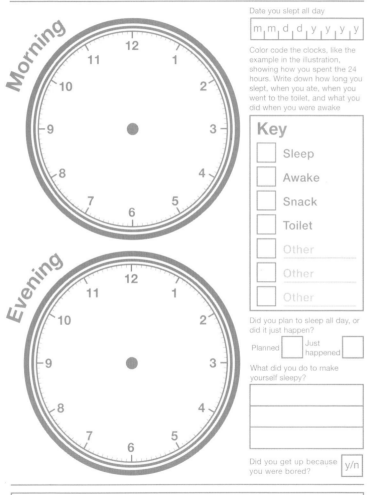

Morning

Evening

Date you slept all day

| m | m | d | d | y | y | y | y |

Color code the clocks, like the
example in the illustration,
showing how you spent the 24
hours. Write down how long you
slept, when you ate, when you
went to the toilet, and what you
did when you were awake

Key

☐ Sleep

☐ Awake

☐ Snack

☐ Toilet

☐ Other

☐ Other

☐ Other

Did you plan to sleep all day, or
did it just happen?

Planned ☐   Just happened ☐

What did you do to make
yourself sleepy?

Did you get up because
you were bored?   y/n

At the same time, you could complete these **Things to Do**
5: Keep a Dream Diary
20: Stay Up All Night • 49: Read These Books

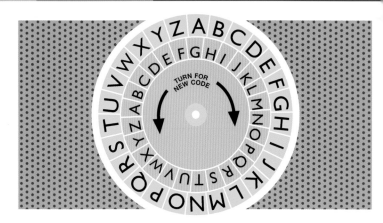

Invent a Secret Code

While you may want to share your secrets with a few trusted friends, certain busybodies (including parents and teachers) should be prevented from finding them out at all costs! Keep your confidential information strictly between you and your friends by inventing a secret code.

Zkdw Grhv Wklv Vdb?

- The most basic way to create a code is to swap around the letters in the alphabet (or swap letters for numbers). A code wheel will help you do this. Cut out two circles from cardstock, but make one a couple of inches smaller in diameter than the other. Write the alphabet around the perimeter of each circle, and attach the smaller one to the larger one using a paper fastener (see illustration above). Turn the inner wheel to pick a new code. To make the code harder, write the letters in a random order (not alphabetical) on the inner wheel. If you want to use numbers instead (or a mixture of both), write these in place of the letters on the inner wheel.
- Don't go for anything too obvious like A=Z, B=Y, C=X, and so on, or A=1, B=2, C=3, and so on. Code breakers are bound to check these first. However, it does help to choose one that's memorable. Change your code frequently to put potential code breakers off the scent, but make sure your friends know when you're doing this so they can adjust their code wheel to match yours!

Make your own invisible ink: Write a message in lemon juice or milk and wait for it to dry. When it's dry, the message will disappear. To make it reappear, wave it over a candle or heat it up in the oven. Be careful not to burn your secret message though!

Invent a Secret Code **Form**

Once you have completed this **Thing to Do**,
stick your Achieved Star here and fill in the form

Achieved

The Original Caesar Cipher

USE THIS CODE TO
DECIPHER ENCRYPTED
PARTS OF THIS BOOK

Julius Caesar used the
code below in 50 BC!

Try it out, but be
warned—it isn't one
of the hardest to crack!

You can do much
better than Caesar!

A = D	N = Q
B = E	O = R
C = F	P = S
D = G	Q = T
E = H	R = U
F = I	S = V
G = J	T = W
H = K	U = X
I = L	V = Y
J = M	W = Z
K = N	X = A
L = O	Y = B
M = P	Z = C

Your codes: Make a note of your secret codes here. Make sure you
have more than one code to confuse any would-be code breakers

CODE ONE

A =	B =	C =	D =	E =	F =
G =	H =	I =	J =	K =	L =
M =	N =	O =	P =	Q =	R =
S =	T =	U =	V =	W =	X =
Y =	Z =	1 =	2 =	3 =	4 =
5 =	6 =	7 =	8 =	9 =	0 =
=	=	=	=	=	=

CODE TWO

A =	B =	C =	D =	E =	F =
G =	H =	I =	J =	K =	L =
M =	N =	O =	P =	Q =	R =
S =	T =	U =	V =	W =	X =
Y =	Z =	1 =	2 =	3 =	4 =
5 =	6 =	7 =	8 =	9 =	0 =
=	=	=	=	=	=

CODE THREE

A =	B =	C =	D =	E =	F =
G =	H =	I =	J =	K =	L =
M =	N =	O =	P =	Q =	R =
S =	T =	U =	V =	W =	X =
Y =	Z =	1 =	2 =	3 =	4 =
5 =	6 =	7 =	8 =	9 =	0 =
=	=	=	=	=	=

At the same time, you could complete these **Things to Do**
74: Become a Spy • 76: Learn to Say Useful Phrases in Other Languages
80: Start Your Own Secret Society

Learn to Do a Card Trick

Fool your friends into thinking you have magical talents. Whatever you do, don't give away the secrets of your card tricks.

It's a Kind of Magic

Here are two deceptively simple card tricks for you to try out:

1. Lay down 16 cards in 4 rows of 4. Ask your spectator to pick a card but not to tell you which. Ask them which row it's in: A, B, C, or D (e.g., B) [1]. Start replacing the cards one by one onto the top of the deck in a seemingly random order, but make sure every fourth card you pick up is from the row they said. Lay the 16 cards down again and you'll find that the 4 cards from that row are now at the start of each row [2]. So when you ask them again which row their card is in, it will be the first card in that row. Now that you know their card, you can shuffle as much as you want. Turn the cards over one by one until you get to their card.

2. Get your victim to pick any card from the pack. Ask them to put it on top of the deck. Cut the deck and find their card. All you need to do is see what the bottom card on the pack is. So idly shuffle the pack, glancing down to see the bottom card. Fan the pack and ask your victim to pick a card. Gather the cards together and ask them to put the card on the top of the pack. Next ask them to cut the pack and place the bottom half of the cards onto the top half. Now take the cards and start turning them over one by one. When you see the bottom card appear, the next card is theirs.

That's magic!

Playing cards were invented by the Chinese in the tenth century but didn't resemble the cards we know today. They were imported into Europe by the French in the fourteenth century, where later the familiar suits of spades, diamonds, clubs, and hearts evolved.

Learn to Do a Card Trick **Form**

Once you have completed this **Thing to Do**,
stick your Achieved Star here and fill in the form

Achieved

Trick one diagrams

[1]

[2]

Trick one

How quickly did you pick up the trick?

Slowly [ ]   Quite quickly [ ]   Right away [ ]

How many times were you able to fool your spectators?   `0 0`

What was your average success rate?
Circle the percentage below

10 , 20 , 30 , 40 , 50 , 60 , 70 , 80 , 90 , 100

Did anybody guess how it was done?   y/n

Did you tell anyone how it was done?   y/n

If yes, how many people?   `0 0`

Do you know any other card tricks?   y/n

How many do you know?   `0 0`

Trick two

How quickly did you pick up the trick?

Slowly [ ]   Quite quickly [ ]   Right away [ ]

How many times were you able to fool your spectators?   `0 0`

What was your average success rate?
Circle the percentage below

10 , 20 , 30 , 40 , 50 , 60 , 70 , 80 , 90 , 100

Did anybody guess how it was done?   y/n

Did you tell anyone how it was done?   y/n

If yes, how many people?   `0 0`

How well do you rate yourself as a magician?

☆ Poor   ☆ OK   ☆ Good   ☆ Very good   ☆ Excellent

At the same time, you could complete these **Things to Do**
18: Win Something • 28: Learn to Do a Party Trick
45: Invent a New Game • 65: Learn to Juggle

Grow Something from a Seed

You could buy yourself a partly grown or fully grown plant, but it's much more satisfying to grow one from a seed indoors and nurture it until it's ready to go into the big wide world. See how long you can keep it alive!

Grow Up!

- Seeds are quite cheap to buy from a garden center. You could get them from a friend's garden or things you've eaten, e.g., avocados,* chilies, and fruit. Seeds from things you've eaten should be left to dry first.
- Use an old plastic food container as your plant pot. Ideally, you'd fill it with proper seed compost from a gardening center, but otherwise you can try soil. Place your seed on the soil or compost and lightly cover with more soil—don't bury it too deep, or it'll never find its way out!
- Keep the soil moist at all times, but don't soak it. Encourage your seed to grow by putting it somewhere warm, and as soon as the shoots have started to peep out, move it to a windowsill where it can get plenty of sunlight.
- When your seedling looks to be outgrowing its container, it's time to transplant it outside or move it into a bigger container. If it's going outside, make sure the weather is warm (spring is best). Get your teenage plant used to being outside a week before transplanting by leaving it out in its pot during the day and bringing it in at night.

---

*Have an avocado? Take the pit of an avocado and push three toothpicks into the sides. Use the toothpicks to suspend it in a glass filled with water so the top part is above the surface. Leave it on a sunny windowsill. After about six weeks it'll be ready to plant in soil.

Grow Something from a Seed **Form**

Once you have completed this **Thing to Do**,
stick your Achieved Star here and fill in the form

Achieved

Date you planted your seed | What did you plant? | Date shoots appeared

m m d d y y y y | | m m d d y y y y

How many seeds did you plant? 0 0 0 | How many seeds grew? 0 0 0 | Did you check your plant every day? y/n

Describe how you took care of your plant

Place a photo of your fully grown plant on the seed packet below

Is it/are they still alive? y/n

If no, how long did it/they live for?

m m | d d | y y

Did you plant it outdoors y/n

How tall did it grow in inches? 0 0 0

Is your plant edible? y/n

If yes, does it taste good? y/n

If no, what's wrong with it?

Did your parents *really* care for your plants? y/n

Seeds

How well do you think you cared for your plants?

☆ Poor ☆ OK ☆ Good ☆ Very good ☆ Excellent

At the same time, you could complete these **Things to Do**
57: Plant a Tree (and Climb It When You're Older)
92: Have Your Own Plot in the Garden

Start a Collection

Most people have a collection in one form or another, even if it's just a jar full of pennies or a shoe box full of letters. What's yours? Erasers? Autographs? Football memorabilia? Legos? Stickers? Frogs? Or maybe it's just a collection of dust in your untidy bedroom.

Finders Keepers

- Collect something because you love it and want as many as you can get your hands on rather than because you think it'll be worth something one day. That's just an added bonus. Your collection should be something you can enjoy now.
- There's plenty of things to collect that don't cost money, e.g., bags, shells, matches, stamps, bottles, and tickets. The more beautiful, interesting, or unusual, the better. You don't want a pile of old trash.
- When you have a lot of one thing, it's much easier to lose track of exactly what you've got, so keep a catalog of your collection. Every time you get a new item, make a note of it with a short description of what it looks like, when and how you acquired it, and how much (if anything) it cost.
- Be proud of your collection. Put it on display for all to see.
- If you get bored with your collection, DO NOT throw it away. Box it up and put it in the attic or under the bed. One day you might like to see it again—or sell it, if it's worth something.

 The toys you own now could be the collector's items of the future: Your books, dolls, or movie merchandise could be worth much more one day, so hang on to them and look after them! Keep the original packaging they came in too, as this can increase their value.

Start a Collection **Form**

Once you have completed this **Thing to Do**,
stick your Achieved Star here and fill in the form

Achieved

When did you start collecting?

| m | m | d | d | y | y | y | y |

What do you have a collection of?

Which is your favorite piece?

How many items are in your collection?

| 0 | 0 | 0 |

Is it an unusual collection?

| y/n |

How much has your collection cost so far?

THINGS TO DO
$

Display your favorite items in the display case below. Take photographs to place over the squares

YOUR COLLECTION

ITEM NAME HERE   ITEM NAME HERE   ITEM NAME HERE   ITEM NAME HERE

ITEM NAME HERE   ITEM NAME HERE   ITEM NAME HERE   ITEM NAME HERE

ITEM NAME HERE   ITEM NAME HERE   ITEM NAME HERE   ITEM NAME HERE

At the same time, you could complete these **Things to Do**
47: Make Your Own Buttons • 51: Save Your Allowance for a Month
and Spend It All at Once • 61: Join a Club • 78: Hold a Garage Sale

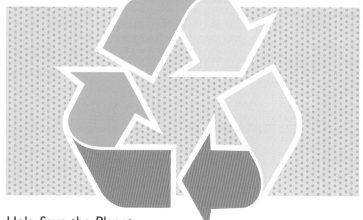

Help Save the Planet

Pollution, deforestation, climate change—these are just a few of the reasons why recycling and energy conservation are so important. For centuries our planet has been misused and abused, and it can't cope anymore. So that's why we all have to act now and do our bit to help before it's too late. Look for the recycling logo.

Waste Not Want Not

- Don't waste electricity. Turn off your computer, TV, and game consoles when you're not using them. Leaving them on standby wastes more electricity than actually having them switched on. The same goes for lights. Turn them off when you leave the room.
- Don't waste water. Don't leave the faucet running while you're brushing your teeth or washing up. Take showers instead of baths.
- Walk and cycle instead of using the car or bus.
- Refuse and reuse plastic bags. Plastic is the worst item to throw away as it doesn't biodegrade. For the same reason, try not to buy things with lots of packaging.
- Recycle your cans, paper, glass, tin, and plastic bottles. There are many more recycling centers for items like these provided by the government nowadays. Find out where your nearest ones are and use them! For organic waste (e.g., food), start a compost heap. It'll be great for the garden.

 Make your school recycle! Encourage them to buy recycled products too. Get your family and friends doing it, and then lobby your local representative for improvements in local recycling services and wider environmental policies (**Thing to Do** No. 84).

Help Save the Planet **Form**

Once you have completed this **Thing to Do**,
stick your Achieved Star here and fill in the form

SAVE THE PLANET CHECKLIST

There is no quick-fix solution to the world's
environmental problems. Are you doing enough to help?

Do you recycle...   Paper? Glass? Plastic? Tin? Cans?

How often do you...   Always Often Some-times Rarely Never

forget to recycle?

turn lights off when you
leave the room?

leave power switches on?

ask for a ride in the car when
you could walk, take the bus, or
bike it?

leave the door open and let the heat
out?

leave the faucet running when
you're not using it?

Have you persuaded
anyone else to start saving
energy or recycling? y/n

Have you ever campaigned
for a greener world? y/n

If yes, who?

If yes, what did you do?

How would you rate your conservation efforts?

Poor   OK   Good   Very good   Excellent

At the same time, you could complete these **Things to Do**
57: Plant a Tree (and Climb It When You're Older)
84: Lobby Your Local Representative • 99: Be Vegetarian for a Week

Turn Back Time

To pull off this feat of mischief, you'll need to use all the cunning and stealth you'll learn as a spy (**Thing to Do** No. 74). The plan is to turn every clock in the house back so your family are late for school, work, or whatever they've got planned. Be prepared for the fact that if you go ahead with this, you won't be very popular for a while. Still up for it?

Time Bandits

- How far do you dare to turn the clocks back? One hour? Three hours? If you prefer, you could put the clocks forward—this is slightly kinder to everyone, as at least they won't be late for anything!
- Wait until everyone in the house is asleep, and then start your stealth mission. Creep into each bedroom and change the time on the alarm clocks, cell phones, and watches. Then progress through the other rooms, making sure you get everything that tells the time. Don't forget the oven, VCR, and DVD-player displays.
- You'll probably only have one chance to get this right because if you get caught in your parents' bedroom in the middle of the night, it won't be easy to explain what you're doing there. So sshhhh!
- Mission accomplished? Then return to bed and get up at your normal time. If all goes to plan, you'll be up and out before anyone else is awake. Prepare for fireworks when you get home.

Films & TV Shows featuring time travel: *The Time Machine* • *Time Bandits* • *Bill and Ted's Excellent Adventure / Bogus Journey* • *Harry Potter and the Prisoner of Azkaban* • *Star Trek* TV series and films • *Doctor Who* • *Red Dwarf* • The *Back to the Future* trilogy

Turn Back Time **Form**

Once you have completed this **Thing to Do**,
stick your Achieved Star here and fill in the form

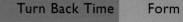

Achieved

Date you turned the clocks back or forward?

| m | m | d | d | y | y | y | y |

What time did
everyone go to bed? | : |

Was it a fight to
stay awake? | y/n |

What was the real time when you changed
the clocks?

What time did you change the clocks to?

Did you get caught snooping around
the bedrooms? | y/n |

Did you get into a lot of trouble? | y/n |

If yes, what happened?

Did you manage to change all the
clocks without getting caught? | y/n |

If yes, how many clocks did you have
to change? | 0 , 0 |

Who did you manage to make late/early?

Dad ☐ Mom ☐ Brother ☐ Sister ☐ Yourself ☐ Other ☐

What time did they wake up
in the morning? | : |

What were they late/early for?

At the same time, you could complete these **Things to Do**
16: Make a Swear Box • 21: Sleep All Day
42: April Fool Someone • 88: Blame Someone Else

Learn to Do a Party Trick

A party trick involves doing something no one else can do. Discover a hidden talent that you have, and use it to entertain and impress your friends.

Get This Party Started

- Many party tricks are based upon people's abilities to do things with their bodies that most of us can't, like wiggling ears (even more impressive if you can wiggle one at a time!). Are you double-jointed? Can you hang spoons from your nose or tie a knot in a cherry stem just using your tongue? How about something grosser, like blowing bubbles with spit, turning your eyelids inside out, or making your eyes bulge out—all utterly useless but entertaining gifts. These talents tend to be hidden. You might not know if you can do them until you try.
- What skills do you already have that you could put together to create something new? For example, if you can play the violin and you can stand on your head, why not try to do the two at the same time?
- You might want to start developing a very impressive talent that others greatly admire and find entertaining or amusing, such as human beatboxing, rapping, doing the robot, or doing impressions of famous people. These will need a lot of practice though!
- Your party trick could even be one of the **Things to Do** from this book, e.g., origami, animal impersonations, or card tricks.

Once you discover your party trick, don't show people how it's done or ever reveal how hard you had to practice to get it right. The whole point is that it is a talent unique to you. If you give your secrets away, then the magic is gone.

Learn to Do a Party Trick **Form**

Once you have completed this **Thing to Do**,
stick your Achieved Star here and fill in the form

Achieved

Place a photograph here of yourself unsuccessfully performing your party trick

What is your party trick?

Did your party trick come naturally? `y/n`

How long did it take you to perfect?

`y y`   `m m`   `d d`

What, if any, accidents happened while performing the trick?

Do you know anyone else who can do it? `y/n`

If yes, can they do it better than you? `y/n`

Date you premiered your trick

`m m d d y y y y`

Where did you premiere your trick?

How well did your trick go over?

OK   Well   Very well   Brilliantly

☐   ☐   ☐   ☐

Did people want to learn your trick? `y/n`

Did you tell them how it's done? `y/n`

Place a photograph here of yourself successfully performing your party trick

At the same time, you could complete these **Things to Do**
15: Fart and Burp • 23: Learn to Do a Card Trick
31: Host a Party • 65: Learn to Juggle

Climb to the Top of a Mountain

A mountain is a mass of land that is over 2,000 ft (610 meters) in height, so you don't have to climb Everest to complete this challenge. A small mountain will do. One fifth of the world's surface is covered by mountains, and while many are underwater in the ocean, hopefully you won't have too much trouble finding one on land and not too far from you.

Running up That Hill

- An ordnance-survey map will show you where hilly areas of land are and the height of the peaks. If you live in a particularly flat area of the country, a trip to Wales, Scotland, or the north of England will present you with many more options!
- Tell people where you're going and when you expect to be back. If you're new to mountain climbing, choose a mountain with an easy, walkable route to the top. Ask a local guide to advise you.
- Make sure you have a map, provisions, and a first-aid kit. Wear comfortable clothes and take plenty of layers—it can get cold at the top. Walking boots and a waterproof jacket are also essential.

Highest Mountain

...in the USA
McKinley, Alaska
20,320 ft (6,193 m)

...in Great Britain
Ben Nevis, Scotland
4,406 ft (1,343 m)

...in Europe
Elberus, Russia
18,481 ft (5,633 m)

...in Africa
Kilimanjaro, Tanzania
19,340 ft (5,895 m)

... in South America
Aconcagua, Chile
22,835 ft (6,962 m)

...in the world
Everest, Tibet/Nepal
29,036 ft (8,848 m)

The REAL highest mountain: Mountains are measured from sea level upward, but if they were measured from their base, Mauna Kea, a volcano on Hawaii, would be the biggest. From its base underwater it measures 33,465 ft. (10,200 m.)—a mile taller than Everest.

Climb to the Top of a Mountain **Form**

Once you have completed this **Thing to Do**,
stick your Achieved Star here and fill in the form

Achieved

Date you climbed the mountain

| m | m | d | d | y | y | y | y |

Which mountain did you climb?

How high is
the mountain? | 0 | 0 | 0 | 0 | ft/m

Did you make it to the
top of the mountain?   y/n

If no, mark on the mountain
how far up you got

Who climbed with you?

How long did it take to climb?

| 0 | 0 | Days | 0 | 0 | Hours | 0 | 0 | Mins |

What were the weather
conditions like?

☀   ☁   ☁☁   ⚡   ➶   ❄

Did you have any accidents
on the way up/down?   y/n

Did you get lost?   y/n

If yes, what happened?

Did you remember to bring
the right equipment?   y/n

If no, what did you forget?

At the same time, you could complete these **Things to Do**
30: Make a One-Minute Movie • 32: Visit…
43: Do Something Charitable • 97: Learn to Take Great Photos

Make a One-Minute Movie

Most directors start their careers making short films. They are a good way to experiment with ideas, finding out what works and what doesn't without spending the heap of cash a longer film would need.

Lights, Camera, Action!

- You shouldn't have a problem finding something to film your movie with. These days there are so many devices with image-capturing capabilities, from digital cameras to cell phones. If you don't have one of these devices, borrow one from somebody.
- Action, comedy, romance? What will your film be about? Look to your own experience for inspiration, such as a dream, a football match, or a fun day out. How about *A Day in the Life of…*, in one minute? Keep the idea simple—a minute is not very long to tell a story.
- Look around for a visually exciting location in which to set your film, and find some interesting props. This might help you come up with a good idea for the plot too.
- Base your characters on people you know, and don't include too many or it'll get complicated. Look at the people around you: the way your family gets on your nerves or your best friend helps you out of trouble. Get them to star as themselves.
- Make a cameo appearance. This is when you appear very briefly in the movie yourself—lots of directors have done this. Don't let the other actors steal all the glory!

 Feeling ambitious? If you enjoyed making your first short film and want to do more, then check out www.nyfa.com. This is UK site where you'll find advice on how to get involved in more filmmaking projects.

Make a One-Minute Movie **Form**

Once you have completed this **Thing to Do**,
stick your Achieved Star here and fill in the form

Achieved

Storyboard your movie here

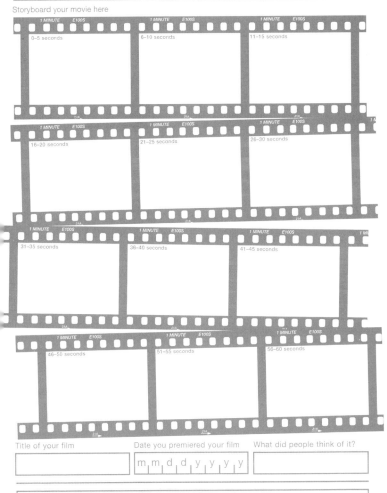

0–5 seconds

6–10 seconds

11–15 seconds

16–20 seconds

21–25 seconds

26–30 seconds

31–35 seconds

36–40 seconds

41–45 seconds

46–50 seconds

51–55 seconds

56–60 seconds

Title of your film

Date you premiered your film

m m d d y y y y

What did people think of it?

At the same time, you could complete these **Things to Do**
17: Act in a Play
48: Watch These Films

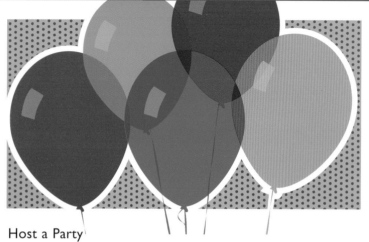

Host a Party

There are plenty of reasons to have a party: holidays, saints' days, festivals, and birthdays (and not just your own—surprise someone!). But you shouldn't need an excuse for one. Just celebrate being young and exciting!

24-Hour Party People

- Try to lose the parents. Tell them to go out and have their own fun. They have to learn to trust you by letting you host the party on your own. Prove to them that you are responsible enough.
- Decide what kind of party you want. Themed parties that involve dressing up can be great fun (see the box below). Or for a smaller event, how about a murder-mystery party or a Victorian tea party?
- Make a list of invitees, and send out RSVP invitations in advance. Having an idea of numbers will help you plan the catering.
- Prepare party food, drink, music, and games, taking into consideration the theme or occasion. Play silly games like sandwich roulette, where you make six different sandwiches, putting something truly horrible in one (e.g., jelly with chilies). The person who picks that one must eat it. Technology permitting, dance mats and karaoke are winners at parties. Twister™, truth or dare, charades, and spin the bottle are classics.
- Study the form opposite for a full list of party host duties. It's a tough job, so make sure you can enjoy yourself too by getting friends to help.

Party themes: Your favorite TV show or book • Superheroes • Movie stars • Cartoon characters • Heroes and villains • Pop stars • Pirates • A period in history (e.g., Romans, Egyptians, the Wild West, 1970s, 1980s) • A place (e.g., India, France, Italy, outer space!)

Host a Party Form

Once you have completed this **Thing To Do**,
stick your Achieved Star here and fill in the form

Achieved

Date and time of your party

| m | m | d | d | y | y | y | y | | : |

What was the party for?

Your birthday | Someone else's b'day | A holiday or festival | Passing an exam | Fun | Other

If other, please specify

Was there a theme? If so, what was it?

Super-heroes | Pop stars | Movie stars | Pirates | Robots | Other

If other, please specify

What games did you play?

Sandwich roulette | Truth or dare | Charades | Spin the bottle | Twister | Other

If other, please specify

If you played sandwich roulette,
did you get the nasty sandwich?   y/n

If you played truth or dare,
did you let out an embarrassing secret?   y/n

If you played spin the bottle,
did you kiss someone you wanted to?   y/n

Also, if you played spin the bottle,
did you kiss someone you didn't want to?   y/n

CHECKLIST OF HOST DUTIES

Did you...

- [ ] welcome guests at the door?
- [ ] check invitees?
- [ ] take coats & bags?
- [ ] offer guests food & drink?
- [ ] organize games & entertainment?
- [ ] organize music?
- [ ] monitor sound levels?

Did you get rid of...

- [ ] spillages?
- [ ] clogged toilets?
- [ ] angry neighbors?
- [ ] unwanted guests?
- [ ] illegal substances?

How many people
came to the party?   0 , 0 , 0

Did you cook
the party food?   y/n   Did you run out
of food or drink?   y/n

Did anything get ruined?   y/n

If yes, what was it?

What time did the party
go on until?   :   AM PM

How well do you think the party went?

Terribly | Not so well | Well | Very well | Brilliantly

At the same time, you could complete these **Things to Do**
20: Stay Up All Night
28: Learn to Do a Party Trick • **73: Have a Sleepover**

Visit…

There are thousands of amazing sites to visit around the world, but what about the great things on your own doorstep? Many people go their whole lives without seeing them because they take them for granted. Traveling around the world is something to look forward to as you get older, when you can leave the parents at home.

Wish You Were Here

- Visit an aquarium and a safari park, and see some of the animals you might come across in the wild one day if you travel abroad. But remember to keep it real by visiting a farm too!
- For adrenaline-fueled fun, visit a theme park. Stuff your face with doughnuts and see them again when you come off the roller coaster.
- For historical adventure, visit a castle. Old buildings are far more interesting when you know what went on in them hundreds of years ago. They're great places for ghost hunting too (**Thing to Do** No. 14)!
- Go to your capital city. Visit the places you've seen on the news and on postcards, and look out for famous people. Be impressed by the huge buildings, the millions of people, and the traffic and pollution, and be glad to get back to the calm of your bedroom. Then for contrast, you can find an area of outstanding natural beauty in the countryside.
- Once you've worked your way through the local **Things to Do**, it's time to visit another country.

A few tips: Take your camera and buy a cheap, tacky souvenir to help you remember your visit. Also wear suitable clothes, e.g., walking shoes for the country, rain boots for the farm, and a raincoat for the aquarium (in case you get splashed by a killer whale).

Visit ... **Form**

Once you have completed this **Thing to Do**,
stick your Achieved Star here and fill in the form

Achieved

[1] A safari park

What date did you visit?

| m | m | d | d | y | y | y | y |

Which safari park did you visit?

[2] A carnival

What date did you visit?

| m | m | d | d | y | y | y | y |

Which carnival did you visit?

[3] A fort

What date did you visit?

| m | m | d | d | y | y | y | y |

Which fort did you visit?

[4] A theme park

What date did you visit?

| m | m | d | d | y | y | y | y |

Which theme park did you visit?

[5] A farm

What date did you visit?

| m | m | d | d | y | y | y | y |

Which farm did you visit?

[6] An aquarium

What date did you visit?

| m | m | d | d | y | y | y | y |

Which aquarium did you visit?

[7] The countryside

What date did you visit?

| m | m | d | d | y | y | y | y |

Where did you go?

[8] Another country

What date did you visit?

| m | m | d | d | y | y | y | y |

Which country did you visit?

[9] A capital abroad

What date did you visit?

| m | m | d | d | y | y | y | y |

What is your capital city?

At the same time, you could complete these **Things to Do**
70: Spend Christmas in Another Country • 76: Learn to Say Useful Phrases in
Other Languages • 97: Learn to Take Great Photos

Learn to Bake a Cake

Baking a cake is fun, it's easy, and it's a great way to make a mess. Best of all, you get to eat all your good work.

Pat a Cake, Pat a Cake, Baker's Man...

- Here's a basic sponge cake recipe for you to try. It's chocolate flavored, but once you've got the hang of how to make it, you can experiment with different flavors, fillings, and toppings.
- Other flavors to try: lemon or orange (add the juice and rind), banana (mash it up), carrot (grated), vanilla essence, coffee (add a bit of instant coffee mixed with water), ginger, molasses, or cinnamon.
- Fillings to try: jam, lemon curd, fresh or cooked fruit, whipped cream, sweetened cream cheese, or icing (mix confectioners' sugar with butter/margarine, and flavor with anything you like!).
- Toppings to try: icing (add colorings if you want to get artistic), nuts, chocolate, fruit, sprinkles, small candies, marzipan, confectioners' sugar, and candied cherries. See how many different ones you can get on!

Ingredients

4 oz (100 g) butter/marge
4 oz (100 g) extra-fine sugar
2 eggs, beaten
2 oz (50 g) cocoa powder
4 oz (100 g) self-raising flour

Method

Cream the butter and sugar (an electric mixer will do the job much faster than a wooden spoon) until the mixture's light and fluffy. Add the eggs little by little, mixing in between, and then fold in the flour and cocoa. Spoon the mixture into a greased and lined 7 in. cake pan. Level the surface and bake in a preheated oven at 350°F (180°C) for 25–30 mins. To test if the cake is ready, insert a fork. If it comes out clean, it's done! Wait for the cake to cool before turning it out onto a rack.

Homemade cakes make great gifts too: Decorate or shape your cake to suit the person you're giving it to and the occasion (e.g., a red, heart-shaped cake for St. Valentine's Day). Only give it to the sort of people who will share it with you—like your grandma!

Learn to Bake a Cake **Form**

Once you have completed this **Thing to Do**,
stick your Achieved Star here and fill in the form

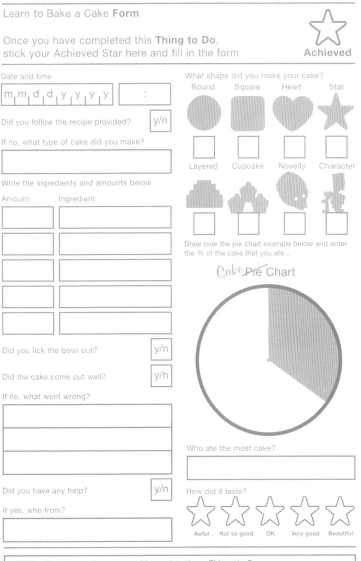

Achieved

Date and time

| m m d d y y y y | : |

Did you follow the recipe provided?   y/n

If no, what type of cake did you make?

Write the ingredients and amounts below

| Amount | Ingredient |

Did you lick the bowl out?   y/n

Did the cake come out well?   y/n

If no, what went wrong?

Did you have any help?   y/n

If yes, who from?

What shape did you make your cake?

Round   Square   Heart   Star

Layered   Cupcake   Novelty   Character

Draw over the pie chart example below and enter
the % of the cake that you ate...

Cake Pie Chart

Who ate the most cake?

How did it taste?

Awful   Not so good   OK   Very good   Beautiful

At the same time, you could complete these **Things to Do**
31: Host a Party • 62: Cook a Meal
71: Do Something Nice without Being Asked • 95: Make a Unique Milk Shake

Hide a Treasure and Leave a Map for Friends to Find

It'd be great to find your fortune in buried treasure, but it's probably not going to happen. Still, you can have plenty of fun setting up a treasure hunt for your best friends. Just make sure they return the favor one day!

Treasure Hunt

- First draw your treasure map, making sure you include all the most significant landmarks so that your friends can work out where they are and where they need to go.
- If you want to be really clever, leave a riddle where X marks the spot. When the riddle is solved, the precise location of the treasure is revealed. For example, say the map leads to your grandparents' living room. You could leave the following riddle: "When does 1=5 and 5=20?" (answer = on a clock). Then hide the treasure in the grandfather clock. Leaving a series of puzzles that reveal clues to the location of the treasure will make the hunt more difficult and fun.
- Put items in the treasure chest that you know your friends (and you!) will like. Then fill it with chocolate coins to give the impression of real treasure. If you're burying your treasure, make sure it's sealed in a waterproof container.
- Hide the map outside in a bottle where your friends can "accidentally" stumble across it. But hide your treasure well. Only the map owner should be able to find it!

 To make your map look authentic and old, soak it in tea and dry it out on a radiator. Be careful not to burn it though, and make sure it's still readable.

Hide a Treasure and Leave a Map
for Friends to Find **Form**
Once you have completed this **Thing to Do**,
stick your Achieved Star here and fill in the form

Achieved

Treasure Map

In the space provided below, draw the route to
your treasure chest. X marks the spot where your
treasure is hidden. Make sure you add to
the map significant landmarks, like trees and
buildings. Also indicate where puzzles and
clues (if any) have been left.

X

Your treasure here

Who did you make the map for?

How long did it take them to find it?

Did your friends share the   y/n
treasure with you?

At the same time, you could complete these **Things to Do**
1: Send a Message in a Bottle
46: Go as Fast as You Can

My friend has a crush on you ...

Learn How to Ask Someone Out (and How to Dump Them)

Now that you've learned how to tell if the one you have a crush on likes you too (**Thing to Do** No. 4), all you've got to do is pluck up the courage to ask them out.

Life Is a Roller Coaster

- Be direct: Approach them when they're on their own, tell them exactly how you feel, and just ask them, "Will you go out with me?"
- Or be discreet: Write your feelings down in a note and pop it through their door. Or if it's near Valentine's Day, put your message in a card.
- Or be a coward: Get your friend to ask them out for you.

Your bravery paid off and they said yes, but it's time to move on. How do you get rid of them without making things awkward every time you see them? They'll want to know why. You could either tell the truth (e.g., "I like someone else" or "You're getting on my nerves") or, like most people, try to make them feel better by laying the blame on yourself with phrases like "It's not you, it's me," "I need time on my own," or "I just want to be friends."

- Be direct: Don't string them along. As soon as you know it's over, tell them straight out. Like ripping off a Band-Aid, it hurts, but the quicker, the better.
- Or be discreet: Break the bad news to them in a letter. You'll be able to phrase it much more nicely, and you won't have to deal with the fallout!
- Or be a coward: Get your friend to dump them for you.

First-date ideas: Go to the movies • Go to a party • Go shopping in town • Go to the park • Go out for food • Go for a walk or bike ride • Rent a video or DVD • Hang out at home, listening to music • Go to the beach • Complete one of the **Things to Do** together

Learn How to Ask Someone Out
(and How to Dump Them) **Form**
Once you have completed this **Thing to Do**,
stick your Achieved Star here and fill in the form

☆ **Achieved**

Asking Out

Who did you ask out?

Were you nervous about
asking them out?   y/n

If they said yes, are you still going out   y/n
with each other?

Date and time you asked them out?

| m | m | d | d | y | y | y | y | | : |

How did you ask them?

Directly   In a letter   A friend asked   It started   Other
            for you   with a kiss

☐   ☐   ☐   ☐   ☐

If other, please specify

What did you say?

What did they reply?

What was your first date?

Dumping

Who did you dump?

Were you nervous about
dumping them?   y/n

Is it over?   y/n

How long were you together?

| 0 | 0 | Months | 0 | 0 | Weeks | 0 | 0 | Days | 0 | 0 | Hours |

How did you tell them?

Directly   In a letter   Your friend   By going out   Other
                          told them   with someone else

☐   ☐   ☐   ☐   ☐

If other, please specify

What did you say?

How did they react?

Were there   y/n   Are you still   y/n
tears from you?   friends?

At the same time, you could complete these **Things to Do**
4: Learn How to Tell When Someone Likes You (and When They Don't)
91: Send a Valentine Card

Start Your Own Blog

The word *blog* is derived from the word *weblog*. A blog is an online journal where you can record your thoughts, feelings, and everyday activities for anyone in the world to read. Some people update theirs every day, while others update it once a month. It's up to you how often you write.

Getting Started

- A quick and simple way to get started is by using the Web site www.blogger.com (although there are others around if you search the Web). It's free, and you can create your blog from there in minutes! All you need is an e-mail address. After filling out a very simple form asking you to pick a user name, password, and a Web address for your blog, you can start designing and posting your blog right away!
- Write about topics that interest you. For example, you could write about your hobbies, your experiences trying to complete **Things to Do** in this book, your favorite sports team, films, friends, and family—whatever you'd like to share with the world about you and your thoughts on life. Speak your mind. Be yourself.
- Look at other people's blogs. See what they're up to and what they write about. If they interest you, comment on their escapades in your blog and set up a link to them. This is a great way to get people interested in your blog. Hopefully, other people will link to you too.

 You never know who's reading... Don't assume that what you have to say is irrelevant to others—put it in anyway. But keep everything you put in your blog original and inoffensive. Copyright and libel laws apply to bloggers too!

Start Your Own Blog **Form**

Once you have completed this **Thing to Do**,
stick your Achieved Star here and fill in the form

☆ Achieved

Date you started your blog | What is the address for your blog?

m , m , d , d , y , y , y , y | www.

Do you use your own name
on your blog? | y/n

Do you get regular readers for
your blog? | y/n

If no, what is the name you use?

Approximately how many readers did you get

... in the first month? | 0 , 0 , 0 , 0

What do you write about?

Annoying parents | Friends | Pets & animals | Annoying siblings | Holidays | School

☐ ☐ ☐ ☐ ☐ ☐

... in the first year? | 0 , 0 , 0 , 0

Do you regularly contribute to other
people's blogs? | y/n

Sports | Film & TV | Books | Computer games & toys | Anything & everything | Other

☐ ☐ ☐ ☐ ☐ ☐

Write some of the names of other bloggers
you regularly communicate with here

If other, please specify

How often do you write?

Every day | 2/3 times a week | Once a week | Every 2 weeks | As often as you can | Other

☐ ☐ ☐ ☐ ☐ ☐

If other, please specify

Do your parents feel you spend far too
much time blogging? | y/n

Do you feel you spend far too much
time blogging? | y/n

Do you get told off for using the
computer too much? | y/n

If yes, approximately how many hours
a week do you devote to blogging? | 0 , 0

Tell the truth, has blogging become
an obsession? | y/n

At the same time, you could complete these **Things to Do**
5: Keep a Dream Diary • 20: Stay Up All Night
85: Write a Story and Get It Published

Write Lyrics for a Song

Writing a catchy three-minute pop song is a goal for many songwriters—
if it's a hit, those three minutes can earn you a lot of money. For other
people, songwriting offers a way to express themselves.

Going for a Song

- Most pop songs seem to be about love because it's such a strong,
  universal emotion. But that doesn't mean you have to write about it
  too. Music can inspire many different emotions. Think about a personal
  experience or something that makes you angry, happy, sad, scared,
  confused, or dreamy, and write about that.
- As soon as that first line pops into your head, write it down. Some of
  the most famous lyrics were scrawled on a napkin or crumpled up piece
  of paper, and written in the back of a taxi or while waiting on line.
  So grab whatever writing tools are at hand, and keep the lyrics safe
  until you can come back to them later.
- The title and chorus will carry the main message of the song and set
  the tone, so it might help you to write these first. Use the verses to
  build a story around that message or theme. Make sure you grab your
  audience's attention with some outstanding first lines too.
- You'll have more freedom if you write your lyrics like a poem, rather
  than try to fit them around a tune you've got in your head. Having to
  rhyme and write to a verse/chorus structure is challenging enough.

Stuck for words? If you're finding it hard to rhyme, use a rhyming dictionary. There are
plenty to be found on the Internet if you don't want to buy one. And if you get completely
stuck, remember you can always fall back on a few *Oo*'s and *La*'s!

Write Lyrics for a Song **Form**

Once you have completed this **Thing to Do**,
stick your Achieved Star here and fill in the form

☆ Achieved

What is the title of your song? _____

What is the theme of your song? _____

Write your song lyrics here

_____
_____
_____
_____
_____
_____
_____
_____
_____
_____
_____
_____
_____
_____
_____
_____
_____
_____
_____
_____

At the same time, you could complete these **Things to Do**
58: Start a Band • 85: Write a Story and Get It Published
86: Sing in Front of an Audience • 94: See Your Name in Print

Make a Time Capsule

As you get older you'll start to forget how to have fun. This is all part of aging and one of the reasons why people become boring as they grow older. So to remind yourself of the exciting life you had when you were young, bury a time capsule for yourself to open when you're old and boring.

Going Underground

- Choose a waterproof container that won't biodegrade after 20 years underground. Inside the capsule, place photos of you and your family and friends the way you all look now. Put in a favorite toy, a list of things you like doing, a description of what you were up to this week, and a copy of today's paper.
- Imagine yourself when you're much older and opening the capsule. Make predictions about your future self (e.g. what job you do; whether you're married or not; and if so, who to; and so on), and add this to the capsule.
- DON'T put food, sweets, or pets into the capsule!
- DON'T write down what's inside the capsule, because over time you'll forget, and it'll be a much better surprise when you open it.
- You could either open the capsule 20 years later or wait until you have children and let them dig it up. Then they'll be able to see what you used to look like and how fun you used to be. DON'T open the capsule early!

You can read more about time capsules, including the "Nine Most Wanted" time capsules that have been lost around the world, on the International Time Capsule Society Web site at www.oglethorpe.edu

Make a Time Capsule **Form**

Once you have completed this **Thing to Do**,
stick your Achieved Star here and fill in the form

Achieved

Date and time you buried the capsule

| m | m | d | d | y | y | y | y |

| : |

Where did you bury it?

When do you plan to open your time capsule?
Place this label on the capsule so no one opens it early

Not to be opened until

| m | m | d | d | y | y | y | y |

Take a photo of yourself on the day you bury the time capsule [1], and then take another one on the day you dig it up, 20 years later [2].

[1]

[2]

This photograph was taken on

| m | m | d | d | y | y | y | y |

This photograph was taken on

| m | m | d | d | y | y | y | y |

At the same time, you could complete these **Things to Do**
**5: Keep a Dream Diary • 36: Start Your Own Blog • 97: Learn to Take
Great Photos • 101: Decide What You Want to Be When You Grow Up**

Brainiac

Be a Genius

Everyone has the potential to be a genius. You can be a genius in any field, not just math or science, so long as you show exceptional talent in that area. You could be a creative genius, in writing, music, art—even in the kitchen or on the soccer field! Some people are very clever at sums or essays, but they can't mend a puncture or solve crosswords. There are many types of intelligence. Find out your strengths and develop them into genius.

Clever Clogs

- The key to being a genius is the ability to clear your mind of the random thoughts that clutter it, to exercise the brain every day, and to think creatively. Some people are born with more focus, discipline, or creativity than others, but all three can be worked at and developed. Practice using the test opposite, and read or do crosswords to stimulate your brain.
- Left-handers* (1 in 10 people) might have a head start at becoming geniuses because they use the creative right side of the brain more.
- Being clever won't necessarily make you popular with your peers. But don't get down because someone calls you a geek—geeks rule the world! Bill Gates (a left-hander) is the world's ultimate geek. But he's the founder of Microsoft™ and the second richest man in the world.
- Measure your mental ability with an IQ test. The Internet is home to hundreds of these kinds of tests if you feel like giving your brain a workout. People with an IQ of 130 or above are in the top 2% of the population and can join MENSA, a society for bright people (www.mensa.org).

---

*Who's left? Neil Armstrong • Aristotle • Winston Churchill • Gandhi • Kurt Cobain
Leonardo da Vinci • Marilyn Monroe • Pelé • Paula Radcliffe • Brad Pitt • Lewis Carroll
Jack the Ripper • Albert Einstein • Bill Gates • Julius Caesar • Kermit the Frog

Be a Genius **Form**

Once you have completed this **Thing to Do**, stick your Achieved Star here and fill in the form

Achieved

How clever are you?

Try the IQ test below and see how quickly you can solve the questions. If you answer the questions correctly in 10 minutes, you're a genius! If it takes you 15, you're extremely gifted. For every 5 minutes that passes, your IQ rating drops a place. Answers at the back.

Question 1.
Which symbol creates the pyramid?

A B C D

Question 2.
Which symbols follow in the sequence?

A B C D

Question 3.
What is the value of equation 3 ?

1. ❄❄☀ = ●

2. ☀☀☀❄ = ●

3. ☀☀☀☀❄❄❄❄ = ?

A B C D

Question 4.
What is the final symbol?

→ ↑ ← ↓

↑ ← ↓ →

← ↓ → ?

IQ Ratings

40–55
Severely challenged

56–70
Challenged

71–85
Below average

86–115
Average

116–130
Above average

131–145
Gifted

146–160
Extremely gifted

161+
Genius

Question 5.
What is this shape equal to?

A B

C D

At the same time, you could complete these Things to Do
18: Win Something • 44: Teach Your Grandparents Something New
53: Succeed at Something You're Bad At

Take Care of an Animal

Taking care of an animal isn't as easy as you might think. For a start, if it's hungry, you can't just ignore it because you're busy—it can't feed itself. You've got to be there for it every day. It's a big responsibility. If you have a pet, you'll know all about it. And if you don't? Offer to look after a friend or neighbor's pet while they're away, or walk a friend's dog.

Auf Wiedersehen, Pet

- Feeding: Find out what and how often it should be fed. Overfeeding can be just as bad as underfeeding. Leave clear instructions for whoever takes care of the pet while you're away.
- Cleaning: Most caged animals or fish need their living quarters cleaned out at least once a week. Other animals may need regular grooming.
- Exercising: Playing with them and giving them space to run about will keep them stimulated and happy. Dogs need walking every day.
- Don't lose them! Before you let an animal out of a cage, make sure all the doors and windows are closed. Keep dogs on leads outside unless they're well trained. Nowadays, many pets can be electronically tagged, which means they can be traced back to their owners if they wander off.
- A few more don'ts: Don't hassle the animal by giving it too much attention. Don't just leave the animal for your mom to look after!

For further information, check out Web sites like www.avma.org and www.hsus.org or ask at your local vet.

Take Care of an Animal **Form**

Once you have completed this **Thing to Do**,
stick your Achieved Star here and fill in the form

☆ Achieved

Your Pet

What type of animal is your pet?

What is its name?

Did you name it? y/n

When did you get your pet?
m m d d y y y y

How would you describe the animal's behavior?

Quiet ☐ Friendly ☐ Anti-social ☐ Loud ☐ Hyper-active ☐ Mad as a hatter ☐

How often do you play with the pet?

As often as you can ☐ Every day ☐ 2/3 times a week ☐ Once a week ☐ Every 2 weeks ☐ Never ☐

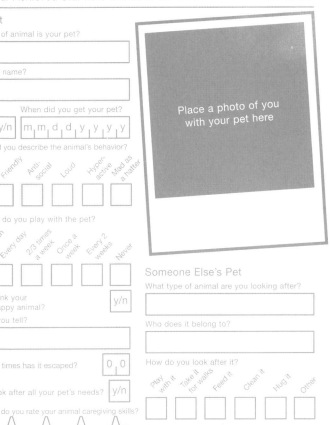

Place a photo of you with your pet here

Do you think your pet is a happy animal? y/n

How can you tell?

How many times has it escaped? 0 0

Do you look after all your pet's needs? y/n

If yes, how do you rate your animal caregiving skills?

☆ Awful ☆ Not so good ☆ OK ☆ Very good ☆ Brilliant

If no, do you leave most of the caregiving to your parents? y/n

Someone Else's Pet

What type of animal are you looking after?

Who does it belong to?

How do you look after it?

Play with it ☐ Take it for walks ☐ Feed it ☐ Clean it ☐ Hug it ☐ Other ☐

If other, please specify

Are you sad to give it back each time? y/n

At the same time, you could complete these **Things to Do**
71: Do Something Nice without Being Asked
75: Watch a Tadpole Grow into a Frog

Learn to Like These Foods

Why is it that the truly awful foods are the ones that claim to be good for you? Perhaps you'd rather eat jam sandwiches for the rest of your life than have a nibble of anything green, anything that was alive, or anything that has come into contact with the carrots on your plate. The thing is, it's actually worth trying to like some foods, because it'll make your life a lot easier if you do. Health is not the only factor. You'll also have much more choice in restaurants, you'll be saved embarrassment when you go to people's houses and they serve something you don't like, and you'll never be denied dessert again because you didn't finish your main course!

Food, Glorious Food

- Remember, the goal is to learn to like the food, NOT to please the person providing it. But if you try something your parents give you and you still don't like it, they'll have to stop hassling you because they can't say you haven't made the effort.
- "If at first you don't succeed…" So the saying goes. It's the same with food. If you loathe something to the extent that you think it will make you sick to eat it, there's a good chance you'll have to avoid it for the rest of your life. But if your dislike isn't quite so strong, it's worth trying that food from time to time, as your tastes are bound to change.
- If you really don't like it, get your parents to sign the form opposite, promising never to serve it to you again! If they break their promise, produce this book and remind them of the agreement.

If you like junk food, get exercising! It might taste great, but it isn't healthy. You'd have to walk for seven hours to burn off a Big Mac™ meal. It's not wrong to have a treat now and again, but you don't want to be overweight and sick as well as old and boring.

Learn to Like These Foods **Form**

Once you have completed this **Thing to Do**,
stick your Achieved Star here and fill in the form

Achieved

Broccoli

Liked ☐   It's OK ☐   Hated ☐
I HATED THIS! PLEASE
DON'T serve me this again.

A parent's signature here

Shellfish

Liked ☐   It's OK ☐   Hated ☐
I HATED THIS! PLEASE
DON'T serve me this again.

A parent's signature here

Lettuce

Liked ☐   It's OK ☐   Hated ☐
I HATED THIS! PLEASE
DON'T serve me this again.

A parent's signature here

Brussel sprouts

Liked ☐   They're OK ☐   Hated ☐
I HATED THIS! PLEASE
DON'T serve me this again.

A parent's signature here

Carrots

Liked ☐   They're OK ☐   Hated ☐
I HATED THIS! PLEASE
DON'T serve me this again.

A parent's signature here

Smelly cheese

Liked ☐   It's OK ☐   Hated ☐
I HATED THIS! PLEASE
DON'T serve me this again.

A parent's signature here

Coconut

Liked ☐   It's OK ☐   Hated ☐
I HATED THIS! PLEASE
DON'T serve me this again.

A parent's signature here

Peas

Liked ☐   They're OK ☐   Hated ☐
I HATED THIS! PLEASE
DON'T serve me this again.

A parent's signature here

Draw the food that you
hate most of all

I **NEVER** WANT TO EAT
THIS FOOD AGAIN!
PLEASE DON'T SERVE
ME THIS IN THE FUTURE!

A parent's signature here

At the same time, you could complete these **Things to Do**
54: Be a Daredevil • 62: Cook a Meal
99: Be Vegetarian for a Week

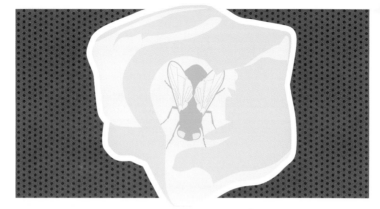

April Fool Someone

Many ancient cultures used to celebrate New Year's Day on the first of April. In 1582 Pope Gregory XIII introduced a new calendar and moved it to the first of January. Some countries, including England and Scotland, refused to change for many years. While France was not one of those countries, many people there rebelled and continued their celebrations on April 1. For this, they were often made fun of. This is how April Fools' Day came about.

Don't Miss a Trick

- Choose your victim. Parents are easy targets, and friends are fun. Teachers are more risky, but if they've got a sense of humor, give it a go. Keep your wits about you though. You want to be doing the fooling and not being made the fool.
- Your April Fool doesn't have to be elaborate, but it's not worth doing unless the victim is guaranteed to fall for it, hook, line, and sinker—and they'll probably be on the lookout. So you have to be very prepared, very convincing, and very sneaky! Remember that your joke is supposed to be funny, not cruel. "Don't dish it out if you can't take it" is the rule.
- There are some hints for practical jokes on the form. Try to come up with an original one if you can though. Make sure you get a photo of your victim's face when they discover they've been tricked (e.g., when they discover the fly in their ice cube). It'll be priceless.

 Ultimate April Fool: On April 1st, 1966, Taco Bell took out a full-page ad in the *New York Times* claiming it had purchased the Liberty bell and renamed it "The Taco Liberty Bell."

April Fool Someone **Form**

Once you have completed this **Thing to Do**,
stick your Achieved Star here and fill in the form

☆ Achieved

Fooling around

Date and time of your April Fool

| 0 | 4 | 0 | 1 | y | y | y | y | | : |

Who were your victims?

Did your joke involve ...

starting a false rumor? · swapping things around? · plastic wrap and toilet seats? · turning back time? · sabotage? · other?

□ □ □ □ □ □

If other, please specify

What was the joke you pulled?

Did the joke go according to plan?   y/n

If no, what went wrong?

How would you rate the joke's success?

☆ Awful   ☆ Not so good   ☆ OK   ☆ Very good   ☆ Brilliant

Place a photo of your April Fool victim here

You fool!

Who fooled you?

What was the joke pulled on you?

Did you feel very embarrassed?   y/n

Did you get revenge?   y/n

If yes, how did you get revenge?

At the same time, you could complete these **Things to Do**
50: Pretend to Be Sick Convincingly • 69: Make a Scene in a Public Place
96: Glue Coins to the Floor

Do Something Charitable

If you've ever thought you've had a bad day, remember that there are plenty of people in the world who have far worse days than you every day. The world is beset with problems relating to poverty, illness, natural disasters, and war. And don't forget the animals. Many suffer cruelty, and in some cases face extinction. Every little bit of money helps. So what are you going to do?

Charity Case

- Pick a charity you believe in. If you love animals, pick a charity like the World Wildlife Fund (www.worldwildlife.org). If a friend or family member is affected by an illness, raise money for their hospital or a related charity. If you want to help those affected by a natural disaster, choose an organization such as the Red Cross (www.redcross.org).
- Fund-raising ideas: Save up your allowance for a month and give it all to charity • Get sponsored to do something (e.g. swim, eat, stay awake, or run) • Hold a yard sale to get rid of all your junk • Organize a date auction • Raise money for charity while attempting **Thing to Do** No. 11 (Get Your School Involved in a World Record Attempt).
- If getting hold of money is a problem, how about donating your time instead? Contact a local charity to see what you can do to help.

Asian tsunami: The tsunami that devastated parts of Asia and Africa on 12/26/04 prompted the biggest charity appeal ever. The contribution raised by hundreds of countries reached over $7 billion (as of 01/27/05). Were you involved in the fund-raising?

Do Something Charitable **Form**

Once you have completed this **Thing to Do**,
stick your Achieved Star here and fill in the form

Achieved

Date you started collecting?

m m d d y y y y

Name of the charity you raised money for?

What made you choose this charity?

Did you participate in a sponsored event? y/n

If yes, what did you do?

Who was your biggest sponsor?

How much did they give you? THINGS TO DO $

Did you give up your time rather than money? y/n

If yes, how?

Did you give any of your allowance you'd saved? y/n

Did you dip into the charity money? y/n

If yes, SHAME ON YOU!

If you raised money in ways other than sponsorship, describe them below on the collection can.

Collection grand total

THINGS TO DO

$

How did you raise the money?

At the same time, you could complete these **Things to Do**
51: Save Your Allowance for a Month and Spend It All at Once
71: Do Something Nice without Being Asked • 78: Hold a Garage Sale

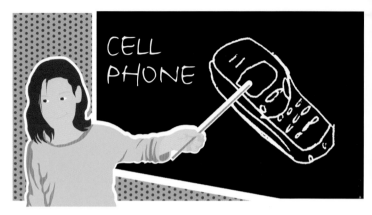

Teach Your Grandparents Something New

They may be older than you, have been around a lot longer, and have more life experience than you, but can they program the VCR? Play a computer game? Or use the Internet? Technology has advanced so swiftly over the last 50 years that it's no surprise many old people are having problems keeping up. You're lucky you've got a fast and eager brain that is more receptive to new information (if you can be bothered to use it), plus you've been brought up with the technology we now take for granted. Things you can pick up in a flash might take the oldies hours to learn. Part of the challenge is convincing them it's worth the effort! Life doesn't have to stand still when they retire—it can get better. It's time to give them a helping hand.

Old Dogs, New Tricks

- Start your grandparents on something simple, like program the VCR or DVD player. Show them how to do it, and then let them try (prepare for the long haul). Don't let them advance on to other skills until you're satisfied they can do that one on their own. If you're one of those people who always likes to win, teach them computer games. If you like a challenge, try explaining to them what the Internet is.
- Test them regularly to make sure that they've been using the skills they learned from you. As people get older, while their long-term memory seems to improve, their short-term memory can be all over the place. You'll probably have to repeat the lessons many times over.

 Nontechnical lessons: Your grandparents might also need guidance on new words, modern music, different cultures, modern relationships, and so on. You might be able to teach them something new, but that doesn't mean they'll change their views or tastes.

Teach Your Grandparents Something New **Form**

Once you have completed this **Thing to Do**,
stick your Achieved Star here and fill in the form

Achieved

How old is your grandma? [0,0]   How old is your grandpa? [0,0]

Who did you teach something new to?

Your grandma [ ]   Your grandpa [ ]   Both [ ]

What did you try to teach them?

[   ]

How well did they do?

Didn't under-stand it at all [ ]   Did OK [ ]   Better than you thought [ ]   Picked it up quickly [ ]   Brilliantly [ ]

Do you think they'll remember the skills? [y/n]

How would you rate your teaching abilities?

☆ Bad   ☆ OK   ☆ Good   ☆ Very good   ☆ Brilliant

The next time you visit your grandparents, test them to see if they've remembered the skills you taught them

Did they remember the skills? [y/n]

If no, did you have to start from scratch? [y/n]

Or did they just need a quick reminder? [y/n]

If yes, did you see any improvement? [y/n]

If yes, how had they improved?

[   ]

Rate your grandparents' learning skills from 1 to 5, 1 being the lowest score and 5 being the highest. How well did they understand...

cell phones?
| 1 | 2 | 3 | 4 | 5 |

e-mail?
| 1 | 2 | 3 | 4 | 5 |

the Internet?
| 1 | 2 | 3 | 4 | 5 |

computer games?
| 1 | 2 | 3 | 4 | 5 |

VCR and DVD players?
| 1 | 2 | 3 | 4 | 5 |

TV and film?
| 1 | 2 | 3 | 4 | 5 |

modern music?
| 1 | 2 | 3 | 4 | 5 |

modern relationships?
| 1 | 2 | 3 | 4 | 5 |

Name 5 things that you've learned from them

1.
2.
3.
4.
5.

At the same time, you could complete these **Things to Do**
9: Play a Computer Game to the End • 39: Be a Genius
45: Invent a New Game • 81: Research Your Family Tree

Invent a New Game

Sometimes board games do exactly what they sound like they do—make you bored! You get halfway through and can't be bothered (especially if you're losing!). So why not invent your own exciting game, then?

Play the Game

- Modify an existing game, e.g., that family favorite, Monopoly™. In your version of the game, why not make the places on the board local streets and buildings? Include your house and your friends'. Try swapping GO TO JAIL for GO TO SCHOOL—and make your own game pieces, maybe basing them on people you know.

- Invent a game from scratch. Design a board on a piece of cardboard (e.g., from a cereal box) and make your own counters. Will your game involve acting, singing, drawing, writing, telling jokes, doing dares, lying, telling the truth, or general knowledge or specialized intelligence tests? Use your imagination, but keep the rules simple.

- Playing cards present endless possibilities for new games. Will yours be a game of luck or skill? For one player or several players? If you're stuck for ideas, base it around existing games, like solitaire or poker.

- Go outside and invent an active game that involves running, a ball, hiding, water, some kind of net, your pet dog, dancing, a wheelbarrow, or all of the above! Think outside the box/court/field.

Invented your game? Then let the tournament begin! Have your friends over and start a league. As the inventor, you will obviously be one of the strongest contenders. Or maybe you'd better act as referee and scorekeeper—no one will know the rules better than you!

Invent a New Game **Form**

Once you have completed this **Thing to Do**,
stick your Achieved Star here and fill in the form

☆ Achieved

Date you invented your game?

| m | m | d | d | y | y | y | y |

What is the name of your game?

How many players can play your game?

Minimum number | 0 , 0

Maximum number | 0 , 0

What kind of game is it?

Board ☐ Card ☐ Ball ☐ Quiz ☐ Racing ☐ Other ☐

If other, please specify

How did others rate your game?

Too complicated ☐ Too easy ☐ Too hard ☐ Boring ☐ Brilliant ☐ Too long ☐ Too short ☐ Other ☐

If other, please specify

Place a photograph of people playing your game here

Write the rules below

Game rules

At the same time, you could complete these **Things to Do**
18: **Win Something** • 23: **Learn to Do a Card Trick**
31: **Host a Party** • 55: **Invent a New Trend**

Go as Fast as You Can

How fast can you run? How fast can you ride your bike? How fast is it possible to go? Have you got the energy and the guts to find out?

The Need for Speed

- Run for it! Sprint 50 or 100 meters against your friends. Ask someone to stand by with a stopwatch to record your best time.
- Get on your bike if running's not your thing. Set a flat or downhill course somewhere free from traffic, and see who can go the fastest. You'll need a bicycle helmet and a speedometer.
- You're unlikely to go over 140 mph in a train in the UK due to a lack of high-speed lines. But France isn't far, and it has one of the fastest trains in the world: the TGV. It can travel at over 200 mph!
- If you really want to get the adrenaline pumping and the heart pounding, go fast on a roller coaster. Find out from the operators how fast the ride goes, then keep searching for a faster one.
- The fastest you're ever likely to go is in a plane, even though it can sometimes feel like you're hardly moving! A Boeing 747 has an average cruise speed of 556 mph. Next time you fly, ask a flight attndant for your top flight speed.

 Traveling fast without moving: The earth is constantly spinning. If you stand on the equator, your speed through space is 1,038 mph. At the North and South poles, it's almost 0 mph. The atmosphere is thicker at the equator, which means you weigh less too!

Go As Fast As You Can **Form**

Once you have completed this **Thing to Do**,
stick your Achieved Star here and fill in the form

Achieved

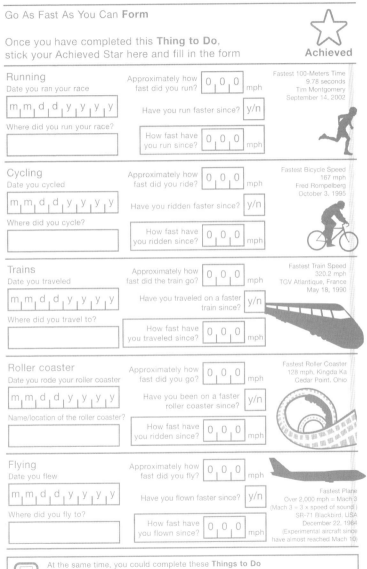

Running
Date you ran your race

m m d d y y y y

Where did you run your race?

Approximately how fast did you run? 0 0 0 mph

Have you run faster since? y/n

How fast have you run since? 0 0 0 mph

Fastest 100-Meters Time
9.78 seconds
Tim Montgomery
September 14, 2002

Cycling
Date you cycled

m m d d y y y y

Where did you cycle?

Approximately how fast did you ride? 0 0 0 mph

Have you ridden faster since? y/n

How fast have you ridden since? 0 0 0 mph

Fastest Bicycle Speed
167 mph
Fred Rompelberg
October 3, 1995

Trains
Date you traveled

m m d d y y y y

Where did you travel to?

Approximately how fast did the train go? 0 0 0 mph

Have you traveled on a faster train since? y/n

How fast have you traveled since? 0 0 0 mph

Fastest Train Speed
320.2 mph
TGV Atlantique, France
May 18, 1990

Roller coaster
Date you rode your roller coaster

m m d d y y y y

Name/location of the roller coaster?

Approximately how fast did you go? 0 0 0 mph

Have you been on a faster roller coaster since? y/n

How fast have you ridden since? 0 0 0 mph

Fastest Roller Coaster
128 mph, Kingda Ka
Cedar Point, Ohio

Flying
Date you flew

m m d d y y y y

Where did you fly to?

Approximately how fast did you fly? 0 0 0 mph

Have you flown faster since? y/n

How fast have you flown since? 0 0 0 mph

Fastest Plane
Over 2,000 mph = Mach 3
(Mach 3 = 3 x speed of sound)
SR-71 Blackbird, USA
December 22, 1964
(Experimental aircraft since
have almost reached Mach 10)

At the same time, you could complete these **Things to Do**
2: **Run up an Escalator the Wrong Way**
18: **Win Something** • 98: **Drive Something**

Make Your Own Buttons

Buttons are a great way to get your message across, as well as brighten up your clothes, backpacks, and pencil cases. Pick a new button each day to suit your mood (and your outfit!). They're fun to design and easy to make.

Collect Buttons

- Keep your buttons small. One inch (25 mm) buttons are the perfect size. You don't want them too big, or people might think you're a clown! Plus the smaller they are, the more of them you can wear.
- You can make your buttons by tracing the designs on the opposite page. If you want a blank button template to practice your own designs on, download one from the Web site (www.101thingstodobook.com).
- Once you have a design, you can make your button using a button machine. They vary in price—the cheaper ones can often be found in toy shops. Alternatively, cut your button base out of cardboard (cereal boxes are good), draw or glue your design on the front, and stick a safety pin on the back. Some lids might make suitable button bases too —and did you know that you can bake a button from a flour and water mixture?
- When you Join a Club (**Thing to Do** No. 61), make buttons for all the members. Make them for your friends too—some with nice messages, others with mean messages (examples below)—and let them pick one at random with their eyes closed!

Get your message across: Pretty and Intelligent • Class Clown • Cleverer Than I Look Escapist • Young and Loving It! • School Rocks! • School Sucks • Genius • Head Case • Expressionist • Mommy's Boy • Daddy's Girl • Lost Property • I Bite!

Make Your Own Badges **Form**

Once you have completed this **Thing to Do**,
stick your Achieved Star here and fill in the form

Use the button designs provided, or if you would like to use a blank template, download one from the Web site at www.101thingstodo.co.uk

At the same time, you could complete these **Things to Do**
19: Make a T-shirt • 25: Start a Collection
55: Invent a New Trend • 80: Start Your Own Secret Society

Watch These Films

The great films are the ones you love more every time you see them. They live with you long after the credits have gone because you're inspired by the characters, the music, the special effects, and the whole emotional ride of the story—taking you through excitement, terror, sadness, delight, and laughter. Some films are especially good at transporting you to worlds you'd love to be a part of. Have you ever pretended to be James Bond, Luke Skywalker, Princess Leia, or Batman? Here's a list of films you should see while you're young, or you might miss out on some of them altogether. They'll make you laugh, cry, want to don a cape and fly.

Seeing Is Believing

- Don't assume that a film will be bad because it's in black and white. Some of the greatest films of all time are black and white, and many of the ideas used in them are reworked into modern films. They may be old, but they prove that not everything old is boring! *Star Wars* is 30 years old, and the first, feature-length Disney film, *Snow White and the Seven Dwarfs,* is 80 years old! If you've seen a remake of an old film, go back and watch the original—they're often much better.
- Set up a film club with your friends. Take turns renting a film from the list each week and watch it at one another's houses. If you don't agree with everything on the list, that's OK—lists are fun because of the debates they cause. If your own favorite films aren't there, add them.

Snow White and the Seven Dwarfs was the first feature-length animation ever made. Some of the dwarf names to be rejected were Awful, Jumpy, Jaunty, Shifty, Blabby, and Dirty. It took over 550 people to produce the 2,000,000 illustrations used.

Watch These Films **Form**

Once you have completed this **Thing to Do**,
stick your Achieved Star here and fill in the form

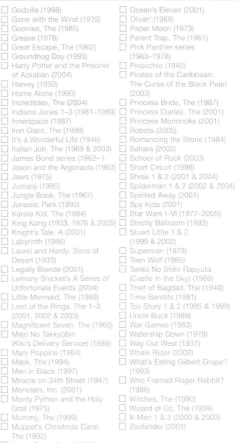

Achieved

- [ ] 101 Dalmations (1961)
- [ ] 5000 Fingers of Dr. T, The (1953)
- [ ] Ace Ventura: Pet Detective (1994)
- [ ] Addams Family, The (1991)
- [ ] Aladdin (1992)
- [ ] Annie (1982)
- [ ] Babe (1995)
- [ ] Back to the Future 1–3 (1985 & 1989)
- [ ] Batman 1 & 2 (1989 & 1992)
- [ ] Beauty and the Beast (1991)
- [ ] Bedknobs and Broomsticks (1971)
- [ ] Big (1988)
- [ ] Bill and Ted's Excellent Adventure / Bogus Journey (1988 & 1991)
- [ ] Billy Elliot (2000)
- [ ] Bringing Up Baby (1938)
- [ ] Bugsy Malone (1976)
- [ ] Casper (1995)
- [ ] Charlie and the Chocolate Factory (1971 & 2005)
- [ ] Christmas Story, A (1983)
- [ ] Chronicles of Narnia, The: The Lion, the Witch and the Wardrobe (2005)
- [ ] Clash of the Titans (1981)
- [ ] Close Encounters of the Third Kind (1977)
- [ ] Clueless (1995)
- [ ] Wallace & Gromit: The Curse of the Were-Rabbit (2005)
- [ ] Dead Poets' Society (1989)
- [ ] Dr. Doolittle (1998)
- [ ] E.T. The Extra-Terrestrial (1982)
- [ ] Edward Scissorhands (1990)
- [ ] Elf (2003)
- [ ] Empire of the Sun (1987)
- [ ] Explorers (1985)
- [ ] Ferris Bueller's Day Off (1986)
- [ ] Finding Nemo (2003)
- [ ] Flash Gordon (1980)
- [ ] Flight of the Navigator (1986)
- [ ] Forrest Gump (1994)
- [ ] Freaky Friday (1976 & 2003)
- [ ] Galaxy Quest (1999)
- [ ] The General (1927)
- [ ] Ghostbusters (1984)

- [ ] Godzilla (1998)
- [ ] Gone with the Wind (1939)
- [ ] Goonies, The (1985)
- [ ] Grease (1978)
- [ ] Great Escape, The (1962)
- [ ] Groundhog Day (1993)
- [ ] Harry Potter and the Prisoner of Azkaban (2004)
- [ ] Harvey (1950)
- [ ] Home Alone (1990)
- [ ] Incredibles, The (2004)
- [ ] Indiana Jones 1–3 (1981–1989)
- [ ] Innerspace (1987)
- [ ] Iron Giant, The (1999)
- [ ] It's a Wonderful Life (1946)
- [ ] Italian Job, The (1969 & 2003)
- [ ] James Bond series (1962–)
- [ ] Jason and the Argonauts (1963)
- [ ] Jaws (1975)
- [ ] Jumanji (1995)
- [ ] Jungle Book, The (1967)
- [ ] Jurassic Park (1993)
- [ ] Karate Kid, The (1984)
- [ ] King Kong (1933, 1976 & 2005)
- [ ] Knight's Tale, A (2001)
- [ ] Labyrinth (1986)
- [ ] Laurel and Hardy: Sons of Desert (1933)
- [ ] Legally Blonde (2001)
- [ ] Lemony Snicket's A Series of Unfortunate Events (2004)
- [ ] Little Mermaid, The (1989)
- [ ] Lord of the Rings, The 1–3 (2001, 2002 & 2003)
- [ ] Magnificent Seven, The (1960)
- [ ] Majo No Takkyūbin (Kiki's Delivery Service) (1989)
- [ ] Mary Poppins (1964)
- [ ] Mask, The (1994)
- [ ] Men in Black (1997)
- [ ] Miracle on 34th Street (1947)
- [ ] Monsters, Inc. (2001)
- [ ] Monty Python and the Holy Grail (1975)
- [ ] Mummy, The (1999)
- [ ] Muppet's Christmas Carol, The (1992)
- [ ] Never Been Kissed (1999)
- [ ] NeverEnding Story, The (1984)
- [ ] Nightmare Before Christmas, The (1993)

- [ ] Ocean's Eleven (2001)
- [ ] Oliver! (1968)
- [ ] Paper Moon (1973)
- [ ] Parent Trap, The (1961)
- [ ] Pink Panther series (1963–1978)
- [ ] Pinocchio (1940)
- [ ] Pirates of the Caribbean: The Curse of the Black Pearl (2003)
- [ ] Princess Bride, The (1987)
- [ ] Princess Diaries, The (2001)
- [ ] Princess Mononoke (2001)
- [ ] Robots (2005)
- [ ] Romancing the Stone (1984)
- [ ] Sahara (2005)
- [ ] School of Rock (2003)
- [ ] Short Circuit (1986)
- [ ] Shrek 1 & 2 (2001 & 2004)
- [ ] Spiderman 1 & 2 (2002 & 2004)
- [ ] Spirited Away (2001)
- [ ] Spy Kids (2001)
- [ ] Star Wars I–VI (1977–2005)
- [ ] Strictly Ballroom (1992)
- [ ] Stuart Little 1 & 2 (1999 & 2002)
- [ ] Superman (1978)
- [ ] Teen Wolf (1985)
- [ ] Tenkū No Shiro Rapyuta (Castle in the Sky) (1986)
- [ ] Thief of Bagdad, The (1940)
- [ ] Time Bandits (1981)
- [ ] Toy Story 1 & 2 (1995 & 1999)
- [ ] Uncle Buck (1989)
- [ ] War Games (1983)
- [ ] Watership Down (1978)
- [ ] Way Out West (1937)
- [ ] Whale Rider (2002)
- [ ] What's Eating Gilbert Grape? (1993)
- [ ] Who Framed Roger Rabbit? (1988)
- [ ] Witches, The (1990)
- [ ] Wizard of Oz, The (1939)
- [ ] X-Men 1 & 2 (2000 & 2003)
- [ ] Zoolander (2001)

At the same time, you could complete these **Things to Do**
20: Stay Up All Night • 25: Start a Collection
30: Make a One-Minute Movie • 49: Read These Books

Read These Books

Some of the greatest books of all time have been children's books. Generations of young and old alike have loved Lewis Carroll's *Alice's Adventures in Wonderland* and J.R.R. Tolkien's *The Hobbit*, or more recently, J. K. Rowling's Harry Potter series and Philip Pullman's His Dark Materials trilogy. This list also contains many great books that if you don't read now, you might miss out on forever, as there'll be other books you think you should read when you're older. As with films, no one will ever be able to agree entirely on what the greatest books are. The joy of lists is debating them and adding to them. But if you're going to Start a Collection (**Thing to Do** No. 25), then these books are a good place to begin.

Read All About It

- Many of these books are films too, so why bother reading the book? Well, the joy of books is that you create the worlds they describe in your imagination, without someone else (like a filmmaker) getting there first. It's interesting to see how the film's vision compares with your own, but often disappointing if it's very different. The order in which you read the book and see the film may influence your opinion.

- Everyone has time to read and everyone can enjoy it—it just takes the right book to suck you in. Keep one by your bedside so you can read a few chapters before going to sleep, and carry one with you to read on trips or while you're waiting for someone or something.

We strongly recommend you read other books by all the authors on the list.
☆ This symbol means that this book belongs to a series.
★ This symbol means that a TV or film version of the book also exists.

Read These Books **Form**

Once you have completed this **Thing to Do**,
stick your Achieved Star here and fill in the form

Achieved

- [ ] Adventures of Tintin, The
Hergé ☆ ★
- [ ] Adventures of Tom Sawyer,
The Mark Twain ☆ ★
- [ ] Aladdin and Other Tales
from the Arabian Nights
N.J. Dawood ★
- [ ] Alice in Wonderland
Lewis Carroll ☆ ★
- [ ] All Creatures Great and Small
James Herriot ☆ ★
- [ ] Anne of Green Gables
L. M. Montgomery ☆
- [ ] Are You There, God? It's
Me, Margaret Judy Blume ☆
- [ ] Around the World in
Eighty Days Jules Verne ★
- [ ] Artemis Fowl Eoin Colfer ☆
- [ ] Asterix the Gaul
R. Goscinny ☆ ★
- [ ] Bagthorpe Saga, The
Helen Cresswell ☆
- [ ] Black Narcissus
Rumer Godden ★
- [ ] Bridge to Terabithia
Katherine Paterson
- [ ] Book of Dead Days, The
Marcus Sedgwick
- [ ] Borrowers, The
Mary Norton ☆ ★
- [ ] Box of Delights, The
John Masefield ☆
- [ ] Catch 22 Joseph Heller
- [ ] Catcher in the Rye, The
J. D. Salinger
- [ ] Charlie and the Chocolate
Factory Roald Dahl
- [ ] Charlotte's Web E. B. White
- [ ] Children of Green Knowe, The
Lucy M. Boston ☆ ★
- [ ] Chocolate War, The
Robert Cormier ☆
- [ ] Chronicles of Narnia, The
C. S. Lewis ☆ ★
- [ ] Cirque du Freak
Darren Shan ☆
- [ ] Complete Nonsense
Edward Lear
- [ ] Curious Incident of the Dog
in the Night-time, The
Mark Haddon

- [ ] Danny, the Champion of the
World Roald Dahl ★
- [ ] Dark Is Rising, The
Susan Cooper ☆
- [ ] Diary of a Young Girl, The
Anne Frank
- [ ] Emil and the Detectives
Erich Kastner ☆ ★
- [ ] Great Expectations
Charles Dickens ★
- [ ] Grimm's Fairy Tales
Jacob & Wilhelm Grimm
- [ ] Gulliver's Travels
Jonathan Swift ★
- [ ] Harriet the Spy
Louise Fitzhugh ★
- [ ] Harry Potter J. K. Rowling ☆ ★
- [ ] His Dark Materials
Philip Pullman ☆
- [ ] Hitchhiker's Guide to the
Galaxy, The Douglas Adams ☆ ★
- [ ] Hobbit, The J. R. R. Tolkien ☆ ★
- [ ] Holes Louis Sachar ★
- [ ] I Am the Messenger
Markus Zusak
- [ ] I Capture the Castle
Dodie Smith ★
- [ ] I Like This Poem: A Collection
of Best-Loved Poems Chosen
by Children Kaye Webb (editor)
- [ ] I'm the King of the Castle
Susan Hill
- [ ] Indian in the Cupboard, The
Lynne Reid Banks ★
- [ ] Iron Man, The Ted Hughes ★
- [ ] Journey to the River Sea
Eva Ibbotson
- [ ] Just William
Richmal Crompton ☆
- [ ] Kensuke's Kingdom
Michael Morpurgo
- [ ] Kite Rider, The
Geraldine McCaughrean
- [ ] Little Women
Louisa May Alcott ☆ ★
- [ ] Looking for Alaska John
Green
- [ ] Machine Gunners, The
Robert Westall ★
- [ ] Mennyms, The Sylvia Waugh ☆
- [ ] Monster, Walter Dean Myers

- [ ] My Family and Other Animals
Gerald Durrell ★
- [ ] Old Possum's Book of
Practical Cats T. S. Eliot
- [ ] Outsiders, The S. E. Hinton
- [ ] Peter Pan J. M. Barrie ★
- [ ] Phantom Tollbooth, The
Norton Juster ★
- [ ] Point Blanc Anthony Horowitz
- [ ] Railway Children, The
E. Nesbit ★
- [ ] Redwall Brian Jacques ☆ ★
- [ ] Robinson Crusoe
Daniel Defoe ★
- [ ] Secret Diary of Adrian Mole
Aged 13 3/4, The
Sue Townsend ★
- [ ] Secret Garden, The
Frances Hodgson Burnett ★
- [ ] Series of Unfortunate Events, A
Lemony Snicket ☆ ★
- [ ] Silver Sword, The Ian Serraillier
- [ ] Skellig David Almond ☆
- [ ] Snow Goose, The
Paul Gallico
- [ ] Snow Spider, The
Jenny Nimmo ☆
- [ ] Speak Laurie Halse Anderson
- [ ] Stig of the Dump Clive King ★
- [ ] Struwwelpeter
Heinrich Hoffman
- [ ] Swallows and Amazons
Arthur Ransome ★
- [ ] Thief Lord Cornelia Funke
- [ ] Thieves of Ostia, The
Caroline Lawrence
- [ ] To Kill a Mockingbird
Harper Lee ★
- [ ] Tom's Midnight Garden
Philippa Pearce
- [ ] Treasure Island
Robert Louis Stevenson ★
- [ ] Tulip Touch, The Anne Fine
- [ ] Uncle J. P. Martin ☆
- [ ] Watership Down
Richard Adams ★
- [ ] Where the Wild Things Are
Maurice Sendak
- [ ] White Fang Jack London ★
- [ ] A Wrinkle in Time
Madeleine L'Engle

At the same time, you could complete these **Things to Do**
20: Stay Up All Night • 25: Start a Collection
85: Write a Story and Get It Published

Pretend to Be Sick Convincingly

Everyone has pretended to be sick at one time or another. If your parents say they haven't, then they must be lying. Sometimes it's the only way to get out of something you really, REALLY don't want to do. Maybe you want to skip school because of a scary math test or PE class, or avoid having to go to your boring relatives' house, where minutes seem to last for hours and you have to be on your best behavior. If you want to win that Oscar, you'd best get some acting practice in now.

License to Ill

- If you know something's coming up that you want to get out of, fake a headache or start coughing a bit the day before so your "illness" is more believable. Don't recover too suddenly either; it'll look suspicious.
- Heating up the thermometer is the oldest trick in the book, but it's a good one. Put it under the hot-water faucet, on a hot-water bottle, or radiator—not for too long though, or you'll be rushed to hospital, which would be extremely embarrassing!
- Pick a common illness that's easy to fake, like the flu, and say there's a bug going around school. Alternatively, go for an illness that's hard to prove, like a stomachache. If you pretend you're about to spew, you'll get sent home in no time.
- Don't be afraid to use props. Buy some green gunge and hang it out of your nose, or draw pink spots on your chest. Burying yourself under a comforter to build up a good sweat is a good trick.

 Don't cry wolf: If you pretend to be sick too often, people will soon catch on, and then they won't believe you when you really are sick. Most things can't be put off forever. You'll have to face up to whatever it is you're trying to avoid eventually.

Pretend to Be Sick Convincingly **Form**

Once you have completed this **Thing to Do**,
stick your Achieved Star here and fill in the form

Achieved

Date your fake illness started

m m d d y y y y

Why are you pretending to be sick?

What did you convince people you had?

Did your family take a lot of
persuading?   y/n

Did you heat the
thermometer up?   y/n

If yes, on the thermometer
provided, draw the maximum
temperature you managed to
heat the thermometer up to

How did you heat it up?

Did they find out you
were lying?   y/n

Grade your acting abilities below

Poor   OK   Good   Very good   Excellent

Were you made to stay in bed?   y/n

Where did it hurt?

Draw on the diagram below the
areas affected by your illness

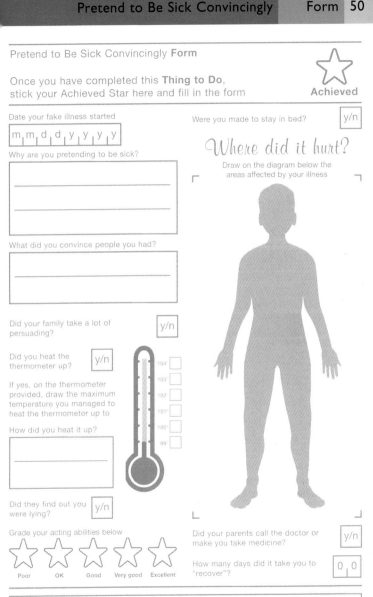

104°
103°
102°
101°
100°
99°

Did your parents call the doctor or
make you take medicine?   y/n

How many days did it take you to
"recover"?   0 , 0

At the same time, you could complete these **Things to Do**
9: Play a Computer Game to the End • 21: Sleep All Day
48: Watch These Films • 49: Read These Books

Save Your Allowance for a Month and Spend It All at Once

There must have been times when you wanted something very badly but you didn't get it, even when you put on your best persuasive charms. Well, sometimes drastic measures are needed—namely, saving up your allowance to buy that special thing rather than making the usual mistake of blowing it on junk food and text messages. If Christmas has been and gone and your birthday isn't for months, you really don't have much choice. Well, unless you've got a soft grandma or grandpa you can work on for the cash.

Money, Money, Money

- How much does the thing you really want cost? If one month's savings won't cover it, do the math and work out how long you're going to have to keep putting those pennies away.
- Consider taking on more jobs around the house or yard to earn some money, or getting a Saturday job or paper route. There are a few moneymaking **Things to Do** too (see the form). It's only for a while, and the extra work will be worth it in the end.
- Keep the money out of reach to help you resist the temptation to spend some here and there. Put it in a piggy bank or a savings account, and ask for your allowance to be paid at the end of a month, not weekly.

How much money goes into your pocket? The average amount of allowance given in the U.S. is $15 a week. If you get less than this, you need to show your parents this statistic. If you get more, definitely keep this information to yourself!

Save Your Allowance for a
Month and Spend It All at Once **Form**
Once you have completed this **Thing to Do**,
stick your Achieved Star here and fill in the form

☆ Achieved

Things to Do moneymakers. How much money did
you make from the garage sale and the swear box?
Write your totals below. DO NOT steal from
the charity money you raised!

Garage sale total
THINGS TO DO
$

Swear box total

Date you started saving

| m | m | d | d | y | y | y | y |

Date you finished saving

| m | m | d | d | y | y | y | y |

How long have you been saving?

| m | m | | y | y | | d | d |

What have you been saving for?

How much
does it cost?
THINGS TO DO
$

Did you find saving ...

☐ easy?   ☐ hard?

If hard, did you dip
into your savings? y/n

How much
did you
take out?
THINGS TO DO
$

*Your grand
total is*

Your savings

What did you buy?

How much
did they give
you?
THINGS TO DO
$

What else are you saving up
to buy?

Did you have enough
money? y/n If yes Did you have
anything left over? y/n

If no, did your parents
make up the shortfall? y/n How much?
THINGS TO DO
$

At the same time, you could complete these **Things to Do**
25: Start a Collection • 32: Visit...
43: Do Something Charitable • 96: Glue Coins to the Floor

Learn to Swim

When you can swim, it's hard to imagine why others can't, because, like riding a bike, it feels so easy and you never forget how to do it. It's best to learn how to swim when you're young because it'll only become harder to learn the longer you leave it.

Start off in the shallow end of the pool, where your feet easily touch the bottom. Next, it's a question of armbands, floats, and a good teacher to help you learn the basic techniques. Monitor your progress in terms of the number of yards you can swim—5, 10 (about the width), 15, 20, 25 (the length of many pools)—and before long you'll be diving for bricks and impressing people with your medley of swimming styles.

Come On, Dive In!

- Floating requires no skill—as long as you have a pair of lungs, you can do it. It's a good thing to try out before you learn to swim, as it proves how easily the water supports the human body and wants to hold you up.
- If you don't know anyone up to the job of teaching you, and your school doesn't provide lessons, then ask your parents to take you down to the local swimming pool and enroll you in a class.
- If you don't like to open your eyes underwater, use goggles—the professionals do. And remember, just because you get some water in your mouth doesn't mean you have to swallow it!

Not your thing? Even if you don't take to it like a duck to water, it's worth having some basic swimming skills, as it could save your life in an emergency situation—or help you to save someone else's.

Learn to Swim **Form**

Once you have completed this **Thing to Do**,
stick your Achieved Star here and fill in the form

Achieved

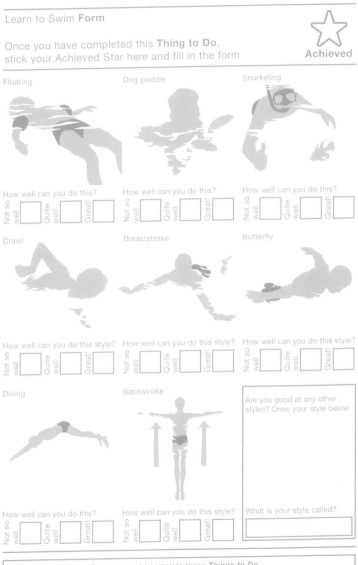

Floating

How well can you do this?
Not so well ☐ Quite well ☐ Great! ☐

Dog paddle

How well can you do this?
Not so well ☐ Quite well ☐ Great! ☐

Snorkeling

How well can you do this?
Not so well ☐ Quite well ☐ Great! ☐

Crawl

How well can you do this style?
Not so well ☐ Quite well ☐ Great! ☐

Breaststroke

How well can you do this style?
Not so well ☐ Quite well ☐ Great! ☐

Butterfly

How well can you do this style?
Not so well ☐ Quite well ☐ Great! ☐

Diving

How well can you do this?
Not so well ☐ Quite well ☐ Great! ☐

Backstroke

How well can you do this style?
Not so well ☐ Quite well ☐ Great! ☐

Are you good at any other styles? Draw your style below

What is your style called?

At the same time, you could complete these **Things to Do**
1: Send a Message in a Bottle • 67: Build the Ultimate Sand Castle
and Have Fun in the Sun • 82: Learn to Skip Stones

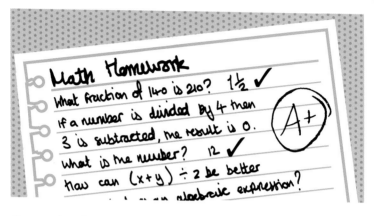

Math Homework

What fraction of 140 is 210? 1½ ✓

If a number is divided by 4 then 3 is subtracted, the result is 0. what is the number? 12 ✓

How can (x+y) ÷ 2 be better ... an algebraic expression?

A+

Succeed at Something You're Bad At

It's a real shame we can't be good at everything, as there's always at least one thing we'd love to be able to do that seems impossible. However, don't ever let people tell you, you can't do something. Brainiac inventor Thomas Alva Edison admitted that genius is only 1% inspiration and 99% perspiration. So if you want to succeed at something you're bad at, you just have to work that much harder at it. But when you finally get there, it'll be that much more rewarding because you did it against the odds. Prove your doubters wrong. Turn a frustrating weakness into an impressive strength.

Do the Math

- Are you too embarrassed to get on the dance floor at the school dance because you don't have the moves? Do you always get picked last for teams in PE? Do your friends always beat you at computer games? Are you bottom of the class in one of your subjects? It's time to turn that situation around. If you're not really bothered, then you won't make the effort to improve, so pick something you'd really love to be good at.
- Have you tried? Sometimes we assume that we're going to be bad at something before we've even given it a go. But if you don't try, how do you know whether you'll be good or bad at it?
- Learning from your mistakes is part of the whole process. In fact, it's necessary in all areas of life. Failure is an inevitable part of the learning curve. You've heard the expression "If at first you don't succeed..." Work at it hard and reap the benefits.

 The only way is up: It's not a good idea to compare how well you're doing with other people's performance. Measure your success by your own progress. Think back to how bad you were when you started. Practice can only ever make you better, not worse.

Succeed at Something You're Bad At **Form**

Once you have completed this **Thing to Do**,
stick your Achieved Star here and fill in the form

☆ Achieved

Before-You-Succeed Report Card

Date

| m | m | d | d | y | y | y | y |

What is the thing you're bad at?

Why do you find it so hard?

Why is it important to you to get better at this?

If the thing you're bad at is a school subject, write your grade below. If it's an activity away from school, grade yourself below

Effort

Overall grade

Achievement

What steps will you take to improve?

After-You-Succeed Report Card

Date you succeeded

| m | m | d | d | y | y | y | y |

How long did it take to improve?

| y | y | | m | m | | d | d |

Was it an uphill struggle?   y/n

What was the hardest part?

Do you feel satisfied with your
improvement?   y/n

If the thing you're bad at is a school subject, write your grade below. If it's an activity away from school, grade yourself below

Effort

Overall grade

Achievement

How have you improved?

At the same time, you could complete these **Things to Do**
8: Learn to Play an Instrument • 18: Win Something
39: Be a Genius • 86: Sing in Front of an Audience

Be a Daredevil

How far will you go to win a dare? If someone dared you to phone your dad's office and ask for Ivor Sorebum, could you resist the chance to enjoy a moment of glory? Fitting a bag of gobstoppers into your mouth is way too easy; ring-the-doorbell-and-run is child's play; running it across people's yards is a walk in the park—is there anything you daren't do? Before you agree to a dare, ask yourself these questions:

Who Dares, Wins

- Have you done it before? If yes, keep quiet. If not, keep reading...
- Will it make you look stupid? Dares are supposed to test your courage, not see how far you're willing to go to humiliate yourself. Don't fall for the dare that requires you to ask out the most gorgeous girl/boy at school. Chances are you'll be rejected and everyone will watch and laugh.
- Is the boy or girl you like watching? This may influence your decision. Drinking or eating something that's sure to make you sick would be a no.
- Are you likely to hurt yourself or someone else? Be brave, but don't be stupid. Don't attempt anything too dangerous. Comedy dares are better than physical dares, and can take just as much guts. If the dare involves another person, make sure that person has a good sense of humor and that what you have to do doesn't involve any cruelty!
- Are you going to get into serious trouble? Trouble with the parents is one thing, trouble with the police is another.

 Dare and be dared: The first rule of challenging someone else to a dare is never to ask them to do anything you wouldn't be willing to do yourself. The second rule is not to hassle or tease them if they refuse. One day you might have to refuse too.

Be a Daredevil **Form**

Once you have completed this **Thing to Do**,
stick your Achieved Star here and fill in the form

Achieved

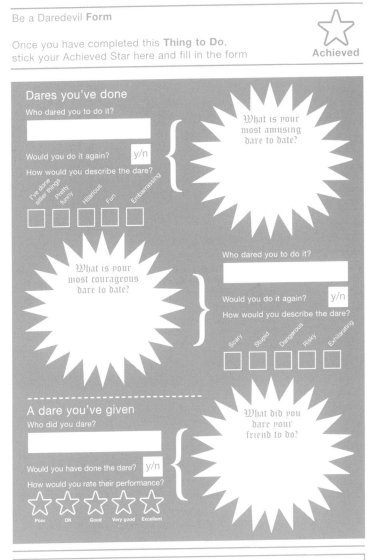

Dares you've done
Who dared you to do it?

Would you do it again?   y/n

How would you describe the dare?

I've done sillier things   Pretty funny   Hilarious   Fun   Embarrassing

☐ ☐ ☐ ☐ ☐

What is your most amusing dare to date?

What is your most courageous dare to date?

Who dared you to do it?

Would you do it again?   y/n

How would you describe the dare?

Scary   Stupid   Dangerous   Risky   Exhilarating

☐ ☐ ☐ ☐ ☐

A dare you've given
Who did you dare?

Would you have done the dare?   y/n

How would you rate their performance?

☆ ☆ ☆ ☆ ☆
Poor   OK   Good   Very good   Excellent

What did you dare your friend to do?

At the same time, you could complete these **Things to Do**
2: **Run up an Escalator the Wrong Way** • 10: **Have an Embarrassing Moment
and Get Over It** • 69: **Make a Scene in a Public Place** • 88: **Blame Someone Else**

Invent a New Trend

Trends come and go. Some last for years (your parents might tell you that they used to do similar things), and others die out after a few days. If you wear a uniform, there isn't much room to be creative with your appearance at school. You have to know how to bend the school rules without breaking them. If you want to start a school trend, be subtle at first, letting your ideas slowly take off. Then after someone else has taken the rap for it, you can claim it was your idea all along.

Trendsetting

- **Clothes:** Experiment with wearing pants and skirts lower, higher, shorter, or longer. Wear thinner ties, or knot them differently, pull socks up or down (or one up, one down!).
- **Hair:** Braids, dye, hair pieces, bangs, partings, asymmetric, scruffy, neat—invent a new haircut or style (school rules permitting!).
- **Accessories:** Start a trend with some unique trinkets—an antique brooch, a necklace from abroad, or a huge ring. If jewelry is a no-no at school, there are other ways to get noticed. What about glasses, buttons, ribbons, scarves, hats, gloves, and key rings? Wear something in a buttonhole or dress up your pencil case or backpack. Find something eye-catching and original, and soon everyone will want one.
- Proving you were the trendsetter can be hard; so make sure you have some early photographic evidence, or no one will believe you.

Actions speak louder than clothes: Trends don't have to be appearance-based. Invent a new game for the playground, a new word or greeting, or get everyone listening to some obscure band. Be confident when doing your "new thing" and watch it catch on!

Invent a New Trend **Form**

Once you have completed this **Thing to Do**,
stick your Achieved Star here and fill in the form

Achieved

Date you started your trend

| m | m | d | d | y | y | y | y |

Is your trend still going? [y/n]

Do you think it will ever come back in years to come? [y/n]

Did your trend involve...

School uniform/clothes?   [ ]
Hair/makeup?   [ ]
Accessories?   [ ]
A new word?   [ ]
Music or a book?   [ ]
Other?   [ ]

If other, please specify

[   ]

Describe your trend in more detail

[   ]

Place a photo of you
and your trend here

When you were the only one doing your new thing, how did you feel?

Stupid [ ]
Nervous [ ]
A bit self-conscious [ ]
Didn't think about it [ ]
Proud [ ]
Very cool [ ]

Were you confident that your trend would catch on? [y/n]

Who was the first person you noticed copying your style?

[   ]

How many people have caught on to your trend? [0,0]

Do people know it was you who started the trend? [y/n]

Did your trend get you into trouble at school or with your parents? [y/n]

If yes, what happened?

[   ]

How cool was your trend?

☆ ☆ ☆ ☆ ☆
Not at all   Not particularly   Quite   Very   Supercool

At the same time, you could complete these **Things to Do**
19: Make a T-shirt • 45: Invent a New Game • 47: Make Your Own Buttons
64: Make Your Bike or Skateboard Look Cool • 83: Dye Your Hair

here...

Place photos of
your friends who
pass the test here...

...and here

name:

name:

Know Who Your Friends Are

The Beatles sang that they got by with a little help from their friends, and it's true. If you end up with the right group of friends, they'll be there to support you through the good times and the bad. Fighting, falling out, and making up again are all part of forming strong friendships (which means even a brother or sister could end up being a best friend!). But be careful, because if you get it wrong, a best friend can quickly turn into a worst enemy—just look at Obi-Wan Kenobi and Anakin Skywalker.

Make Friends, Break Friends

- Best friends will stick up for each other no matter what. Very special ones might even volunteer to take the blame for you. If your friends disappear at the first sign of trouble, you should as well!
- It's difficult for one person to be there for you all the time, so don't limit yourself to just one best friend—have several. This way you can moan to the others when one of them annoys you.*
- A best friend doesn't have to be the same sex, color, or age as you. These are the least important things to have in common!
- Work out who your real friends are before the bad ones get you into trouble or upset you. You don't want to get blamed for their so-called practical jokes or crimes. Fake friends will get bored with you and move on to someone "cooler" one day. If you don't trust them, they're not your friends.

 *Friend envy: While it's normal to feel jealous when you have to share your friends with others, it's best to ignore those feelings or they'll lead to bad moods and fights. If you're the one causing the jealousy, try to make all your friends feel like they're special to you.

Know who your friends are

Know Who Your Friends Are **Form**

Once you have completed this **Thing to Do**,
stick your Achieved Star here and fill in the form

Achieved

Take this quick quiz to find out if your best friends are worth it

Has your friend ever... (X for yes)	Friend one here	Friend two here	Friend three here	How do they rate?
Lied to you?				Add up the number of crosses each friend has scored. Before you judge them, consider:
Stolen something from you?				
Blamed you for something they did?				a) how important those things they've let you down in are to you
Copied your homework/answers in a test or exam?				b) if they're sorry for them
Stolen your boyfriend/girlfriend?				c) if you think you might ever have been guilty of the same. (In fact, you should really take the test yourself before you judge each friend!)
Been in a mood with you for no reason?				
Humiliated you in front of others?				
Played a cruel practical joke on you?				
Criticized you in a way that was not constructive?				0–5: It sounds like they're a true friend. Nobody's perfect, and we've all let a friend down at some point. If you haven't already, forgive them and move on. Only time will tell if they're going to continue to be a good friend.
Borrowed money from you and not paid it back?				
Criticized your family or your house?				
Stood you up?				
Deliberately left you out of something fun they were doing?				5–10: You should probably reevaluate this friendship. See if your friend's behavior improves over time and if things get worse, you might have to start looking for a more loyal friend.
Told other people your secrets?				
Dumped you to hang out with people they thought were cooler?				
Put pressure on you to do something you knew was wrong?				
Boasted to you about something they've got or done?				10+: With friends like these, who needs enemies? Ditch them quickly before they get you into serious trouble or upset you any further.
Not been there when you've really needed their support?				
Refused to apologize for something they did or said to you that was wrong?				
Hit you?				
TOTAL				

At the same time, you could complete these **Things to Do**
4: Learn How to Tell When Someone Likes You (and When They Don't)
22: Invent a Secret Code • 80: Start Your Own Secret Society

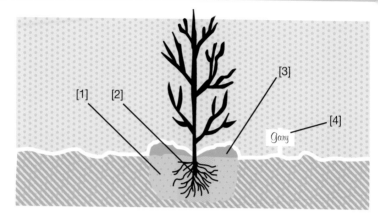

Plant a Tree (and Climb It When You're Older)

Trees are wonderful. By planting one, you are not only helping the environment but also leaving a living memorial to yourself for people to enjoy in years to come—including you. Get planting now so you have your own tree to climb when you're older!

Branching Out

- Choose a location for your tree and get permission from the owner of the property, whether it's a garden, at school, or in a park. Make sure it's not too close to buildings and overhead wires.
- You could grow a tree from a seed (e.g., a acorn or apple seed), but you'll need to start it off in a pot before planting it outside (**Thing to Do** No. 24). Alternatively, buy a sapling from a garden center. Ask for advice on how and when to plant it and look after it.
- Dig the hole twice as wide as the ball of soil around the roots of the sapling [1] and as deep (the soil level should be the same height as it was when the tree was in its container). Don't loosen the ball too much unless the roots are very twisted [2]. Place your tree in the hole, and fill it with soil (and compost or a bit of fertilizer if you can), watering as you go. Cover the area around your tree with soil and plenty of leaves to hold in water [3]. Give it one more really thorough watering.
- Give your tree a name, and place a plaque by it stating its name, who planted it, and when [4].

 Why are trees so important? Trees clean the air by turning carbon dioxide into oxygen for us to breathe. They also provide shade and act as windbreaks, and can prevent flooding and erosion by absorbing lots of water and holding the soil together.

Plant a Tree (and Climb It When You're Older) **Form**

Once you have completed this **Thing to Do**,
stick your Achieved Star here and fill in the form

Achieved

What type of tree did you plant?

What name did you give it?

Did you plant it on
your own? y/n

If no, who helped you?

On the height chart mark the height of
your tree every 6 months and add the date

6 months old

m m d d y y y y

1 year old

m m d d y y y y

18 months old

m m d d y y y y

2 years old

m m d d y y y y

When did it become too high
to measure?

m m d d y y y y

How old were you when 0 0
you planted your tree?

Date you planted your tree

m m d d y y y y

24 feet

21ft

18ft

15ft

12ft

9ft

6ft

3ft

0

How old were you
when you climbed 0 0
your tree?

Date you climbed your tree

m m d d y y y y

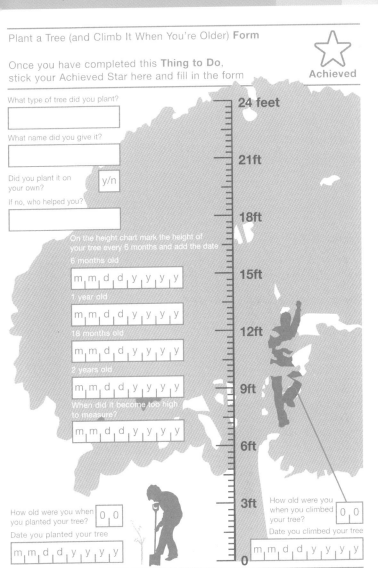

At the same time, you could complete these **Things to Do**
24: Grow Something from a Seed • 26: Help Save the Planet • 34: Hide a Treasure
and Leave a Map for Friends to Find • 92: Have Your Own Plot in the Garden

Start a Band

Do you have some musical friends? Then set up a band. If you don't have any musical friends, then find some quickly (it's your life of fame and fortune on the line here). And if you can't find any, set up a band anyway! Attitude and enthusiasm (and good looks) can get you a long way in the music business. Good luck with it. *TRL*, here you come.

Testing, Testing, 1, 2, 3

- Choose your band name. This is an important decision, as it will be hard to change the name later, when you're famous. Look to other bands for inspiration, but don't copy. It should be original, catchy, and very cool.
- If you did **Thing to Do** No. 8, then you'll be able to play an instrument. But if you can't, then you'll have to be the lead singer. If you can't sing, build that into your vocal style by shouting, droning, or rapping.
- Find somewhere to have a weekly practice. Which band member has the most tolerant family? Do you know someone with an empty garage? Maybe there's a practice room at school you can book.
- Decide if you're going to be a cover band or write your own music.
- You'll either think you sound awful or great. To get an outsider's perspective, record yourselves or ask a friend along to a practice. If you really are bad, you'll need to entertain people in other ways. Dress outlandishly and distract your audience from the music with mad antics.
- Make your debut in a school assembly or concert and you'll immediately have a following of adoring fans. First school, and then the world!

Band manager: Find someone who'd be willing to act as your manager and get you more exposure (you might have to do it yourself). They'd be responsible for entering you into contests and finding you gigs. Oh, yes, and a recording contract would be good too!

Start a Band **Form**

Once you have completed this **Thing to Do**,
stick your Achieved Star here and fill in the form

Achieved

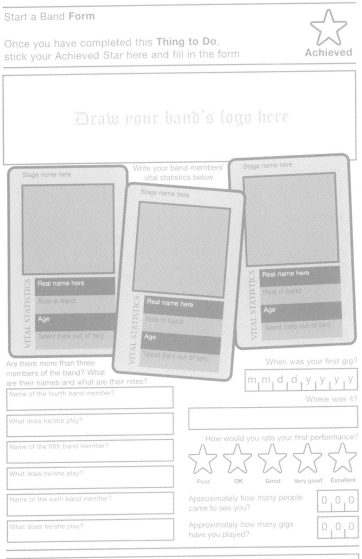

Draw your band's logo here

Stage name here

Write your band members'
vital statistics below

Stage name here

Stage name here

VITAL STATISTICS

Real name here

Role in band

Age

Talent (rate out of ten)

VITAL STATISTICS

Real name here

Role in band

Age

Talent (rate out of ten)

VITAL STATISTICS

Real name here

Role in band

Age

Talent (rate out of ten)

Are there more than three
members of the band? What
are their names and what are their roles?

Name of the fourth band member?

What does he/she play?

Name of the fifth band member?

What does he/she play?

Name of the sixth band member?

What does he/she play?

When was your first gig?

| m | m | d | d | y | y | y | y |

Where was it?

How would you rate your first performance?

☆ ☆ ☆ ☆ ☆
Poor   OK   Good   Very good   Excellent

Approximately how many people
came to see you?

| 0 | 0 | 0 |

Approximately how many gigs
have you played?

| 0 | 0 | 0 |

At the same time, you could complete these **Things to Do**
7: Prepare Yourself for Fame • 8: Learn to Play an Instrument
53: Succeed at Something You're Bad At • 86: Sing in Front of an Audience

Camp Out in the Backyard

It's the camping trip you've always wanted, without your parents interfering and bossing you around. With a bit of imagination (something old and boring people lack), your backyard can become exotic and dangerous new lands. Get your friends together and go on an adventure.

Carry On Camping

- If you're camping on a cold night, imagine you're Antarctic explorers who've become separated from the main group. Watch out for crevasses and yetis! If it's a hot night, you could be in the Amazon jungle, with leeches, man-eating piranhas, and maybe even cannibals to contend with!
- Take enough supplies to get you through the night. See if your parents can be persuaded to let you cook on a campfire (or a camping stove if you can get hold of one). To make it as realistic as possible, you have to forget that the house is there. Don't use it at all. If you need to go to the toilet, use a bush.
- Have fun by scaring your friends. Make an excuse to leave the tent, wait outside for a while before prowling around it, snapping twigs and making strange noises. You can probably flick the tent secretly from the inside to freak everyone out too. When it's dark, sit in the tent with a flashlight and tell each other ghost stories and scary tales.
- If you haven't got a backyard, camp out in your friend's, your grandparents,' or, if need be, your living room!

 Some things you might need: A tent, some friends, sleeping bags, blankets, a flashlight, a radio or CD player, a camera, plenty of snacks, toilet paper, a trash bag, and a walkie-talkie (or cell phone) to contact home base (and order breakfast in the morning).

Camp Out in the Backyard Form

Once you have completed this **Thing to Do**,
stick your Achieved Star here and fill in the form

Achieved

Date you camped out m m d d y y y y

How many of you camped out? 0 0

Who did you share your tent with?

Where were you camping out?

Your backyard · Your friend's backyard · Your grandparents' backyard · The living room · Other

If other, please specify

THE NIGHT BEFORE

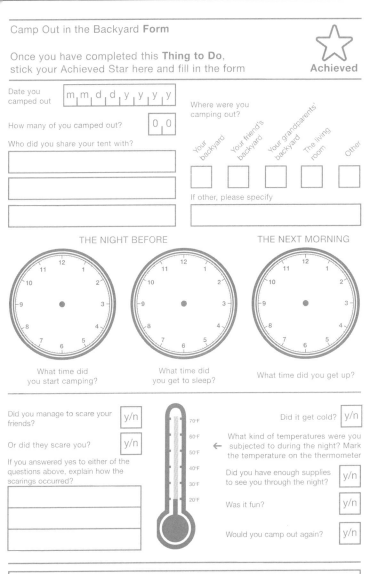

What time did you start camping?

What time did you get to sleep?

THE NEXT MORNING

What time did you get up?

Did you manage to scare your friends? y/n

Or did they scare you? y/n

If you answered yes to either of the questions above, explain how the scarings occurred?

70°F
60°F
50°F ← What kind of temperatures were you subjected to during the night? Mark the temperature on the thermometer
40°F
30°F
20°F

Did it get cold? y/n

Did you have enough supplies to see you through the night? y/n

Was it fun? y/n

Would you camp out again? y/n

At the same time, you could complete these **Things to Do**
6: Touch These Creatures • 10: Have an Embarrassing Moment and Get Over It
14: See a Ghost • 79: Build an Igloo

Learn to Live without Something You Love for a Week

Learning to give up things you love is a valuable lesson in self-discipline. It will help you stick to your New Year's resolutions in the future, and one day you might have to give up something you love that's bad for you. How would you feel if you had to give up watching TV, texting friends, playing computer games, listening to music, or eating chocolate? These things aren't exactly bad for you, but too much of them could make you rather antisocial, poor, lazy, or unhealthy. You need to exercise a little self-control.

Never Give Up Giving Up

- Decide what you would REALLY hate to live without (otherwise you're cheating). If you can't decide, ask friends or family what they think would be the most difficult thing for you to give up (they'll probably be more honest than you!). Then set a date and a time to start.
- Once you know what you're planning to live without, tell your friends and family so they can help you stick to it. If you think you're going to really struggle, perhaps you can persuade one of them to give up the same thing (or something else they love) at the same time.
- It'll be easier to cut something out of your life if you find something else to replace it with. So if you've given up TV, try reading or getting some exercise instead. Rather than texting or e-mailing, write a letter. Or try to complete more of the **Things to Do** in this book. That'll keep you busy. You might just discover something new you love doing!

Need a good incentive to give up something? Ask people to sponsor you while you're living without something you love and raise money for charity (**Thing to Do** No. 43). Or if you give up something that costs money, save that cash up and treat yourself when the week's over.

Learn to Live without Something
You Love for a Week **Form**
Once you have completed this **Thing to Do**,
stick your Achieved Star here and fill in the form

☆ Achieved

Date you gave up TV

| m | m | d | d | y | y | y | y |

Date you gave up your cell phone

| m | m | d | d | y | y | y | y |

Date you gave up computer games

| m | m | d | d | y | y | y | y |

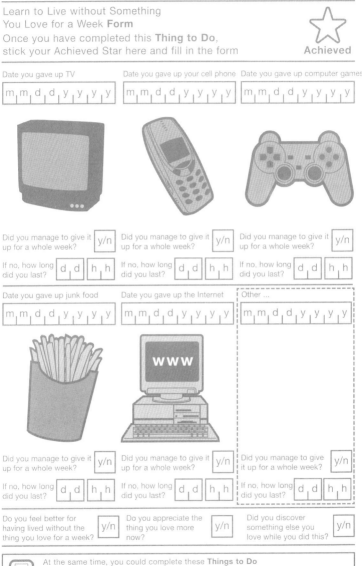

Did you manage to give it up for a whole week? | y/n |

If no, how long did you last? | d | d | | h | h |

Did you manage to give it up for a whole week? | y/n |

If no, how long did you last? | d | d | | h | h |

Did you manage to give it up for a whole week? | y/n |

If no, how long did you last? | d | d | | h | h |

Date you gave up junk food

| m | m | d | d | y | y | y | y |

Date you gave up the Internet

| m | m | d | d | y | y | y | y |

Other ...

| m | m | d | d | y | y | y | y |

Did you manage to give it up for a whole week? | y/n |

If no, how long did you last? | d | d | | h | h |

Did you manage to give it up for a whole week? | y/n |

If no, how long did you last? | d | d | | h | h |

Did you manage to give it up for a whole week? | y/n |

If no, how long did you last? | d | d | | h | h |

Do you feel better for having lived without the thing you love for a week? | y/n |

Do you appreciate the thing you love more now? | y/n |

Did you discover something else you love while you did this? | y/n |

At the same time, you could complete these **Things to Do**
26: Help Save the Planet • 43: Do Something Charitable
99: Be Vegetarian for a Week

Join a Club

Do you have a favorite hobby, sport, game, animal, film, or book? Well, a club's the best way to celebrate your favorite things. You'll be in contact with people with whom you can share information, experiences, and knowledge, giving you the opportunity to make friends with like-minded people. And if you can't find a club you want to join, then start your own!

Go Clubbing

- Look in your local newspaper or on the library bulletin board to find out about clubs in your area. On the Internet you could join a club at the click of a button. Your school probably has lots of clubs too.
- If you're active and like sports, then join a local gym or tennis or sailing club. If you're not the physical type but you still enjoy a bit of competition, join a board-games club, like a chess club.
- If you're artistic, how about a book, art, drama, or film club? Join a choir, orchestra, band, or music group if you're musical. If you like arguing, look for a debating society. And if you like wildlife, maybe there's a conservation group that needs members to help protect and clean up the environment, or you could join a bird-watching club.
- Before you sign up, check out what membership involves. Do you have to pay a fee (and can you afford it)? What do you have to do to be a member? Would you be able to get to regular meetings? Don't take your membership lightly or there's no point!

 Fan clubs: Find out about these on the Internet. Pop and film stars usually have an official fan club and many more unofficial ones. Which offers you the most value?

Join a Club **Form**

Once you have completed this **Thing to Do**,
stick your Achieved Star here and fill in the form

Achieved

Fill in the form below or place your actual certificate here if you have one

This is to certify that

Your name here

is a member of

Write the club you joined here

—————— Club details ——————

Date you joined the club

| m | m | d | d | y | y | y | y |

What is the purpose of the club?

What is your membership number?

| 0 | 0 | 0 | 0 | 0 | 0 | 0 | 0 | 0 |

What are the benefits of the club?

[1]

[2]

[3]

Are you satisfied with the benefits?   y/n

If no, why not?

At the same time, you could complete these **Things to Do**
19: Make a T-shirt • 25: Start a Collection • 48: Watch These Films
49: Read These Books • 80: Start Your Own Secret Society

Cook a Meal

If you want to gain more control over what you eat at dinner, there's only one thing to do: cook it yourself. That way, the person who usually cooks will get a much-appreciated break, and you'll get to eat exactly what you want—and you won't have to wash up either! It's a winner all-around.

Hey, Good-Looking, What You Got Cooking?

- Decide what you want to cook. It doesn't have to be fancy unless you want it to be. Your efforts will be appreciated (as long as you don't poison anyone). Watch some TV cooking shows for inspiration.
- Make a list of the ingredients (and equipment) you need, and check to see what's already in the kitchen cupboards before you go shopping. Make sure you know how to use any equipment properly and safely.
- Practice anything particularly tricky beforehand, and think about how long different parts of the meal take to make. Timing is critical in cooking! There may be parts of the meal you can cook and prepare in advance to make things easier on the day.
- Not many chefs work without an assistant. Employ a friend or brother or sister to help chop, whisk, and dice. As an incentive, let your assistant be the chief taster as well (after you, of course).
- If you want to be very posh, you could design a menu for your meal. Try to make each course sound as mouthwatering as possible.

Too many cooks... Some parents are very protective of their kitchens. You must make them promise not to interfere unless you specifically ask for help. If they ignore you and butt in anyway, tell them they won't get any dessert unless they clear out.

Cook a Meal **Form**

Once you have completed this **Thing to Do**,
stick your Achieved Star here and fill in the form

Achieved

Date and time you cooked a meal for your family

| m | m | d | d | y | y | y | y | | : |

Did you have any help?   [y/n]

If yes, who helped you?

Did you enjoy cooking?   [y/n]

Appetizer

Main

Dessert

Draw each course on the plates provided. Remember: presentation is everything

Menu

Appetizer

Main

Dessert

Coffee

At the same time, you could complete these **Things to Do**
33: Learn to Bake a Cake • 41: Learn to Like These Foods • 53: Succeed
at Something You're Bad At • 71: Do Something Nice without Being Asked

OCTOBER 21, 2006

Dad said, "I'll tell
you when you're
older," today when
I asked him...

List the Things Your Parents Say They'll Tell You the Answer to When You're Older

How many times have you asked your parents a perfectly valid question and been greeted with the standard reply, "I'll tell you when you're older"? Well, this answer is just an escape clause for them. The fact is, you've asked either a question that they're too embarrassed to answer or a difficult one they don't know the answer to! Well, here is your chance to get them to keep their promise.

Only a Question of Time

- The Internet and books can probably provide an answer to most questions, but for the simple explanation, asking someone is better and faster. Anyway, asking questions is a sign of intelligence and curiosity—it's how people learn. That's what parents and teachers tell you—that is until they get a question they don't want to, or can't, answer. Don't let them be hypocrites! No matter how embarrassing or difficult the question, ask away.
- When you hear the reply "I'll tell you when you're older," write down your question, plus the date you asked it on the page opposite.
  On your next birthday (and for as many birthdays as it takes) produce this book and reel off all the questions that you've asked them over the years but didn't get an answer to. See if they're ready to answer.
- Even if you find out the answers on your own, keep asking your parents and get them to tell you anyway. Watch them squirm!

Embarrassing answers: Only ask the question if you really want to know the answer, as there's a chance you'll be the one who's embarrassed by the answer, not your parents. In cases like these, try asking a friend or an older brother, sister, or cousin instead.

List the Things Your Parents Say They'll Tell
You the Answer to When You're Older **Form**
Once you have completed this **Thing to Do**,
stick your Achieved Star here and fill in the form

Achieved

"I'll tell you when you're older!" answers

Write down below the questions you asked, together with the date and your age
when you asked the question. Write their answer in too, when you finally get it!

Q. | m m d d y y | 0 0 | Write the question you asked here

A. Write the proper answer from your parents here

Q. | m m d d y y | 0 0 | Write the question you asked here

A. Write the proper answer from your parents here

Q. | m m d d y y | 0 0 | Write the question you asked here

A. Write the proper answer from your parents here

Q. | m m d d y y | 0 0 | Write the question you asked here

A. Write the proper answer from your parents here

At the same time, you could complete these **Things to Do**
10: Have an Embarrassing Moment and Get Over It
16: Make a Swear Box

Make Your Bike or Skateboard Look Cool

Is your old bike looking rather shabby? Is your skateboard looking as if it's seen better days? Are you in need of a replacement, but you just can't afford to buy a brand-new one? Well, it's amazing what a lick of paint and some well-placed flames can do.

As Good as New

- What look are you aiming for? A supercool sports car? A camouflage stealth bike? Draw up plans for how to soup up your bike or board. Budget for materials, as it's unlikely that you'll have everything you need hidden away in the garage. Look at dragster and racing-car designs for inspiration or other skateboard designs.
- The best way to change the look of your bike or board is to spray-paint it. Make sure the spray is weatherproof and you follow the instructions on the can. Once you've decided on the color, practice your spraying skills on a similar type of metal or wood before doing the real thing. Cut out a template of your design (e.g., flames) from a piece of cardboard, place it where you want on your board or bike, and spray evenly over it.
- There are ways to get a cool look other than spray paint. Try spoke riders (beads which fit on your bike spokes), a colored seat, a pair of handlebar grips, and/or stickers. Reflective tape is cheap and looks great at night. Get some grip tape for your board too—you can cut it to whatever shape you want. You'll have the most blinging transport around!

 The skateboard was invented in the late fifties by Ollie Gelfand as a means of surfing outside of water. Surfers were frustrated by the bad weather and waves. They nailed roller skates to wooden planks to continue surfing. It became known as sidewalk surfing.

Make Your Bike or Skateboard Look Cool **Form**

Once you have completed this **Thing to Do**,
stick your Achieved Star here and fill in the form

☆ Achieved

What are you making over?

Bike ☐   Skateboard ☐

Date you began the makeover

| m | m | d | d | y | y | y | y |

What type of bike/skateboard
do you have?

Was it in a bad way?   y/n

How long have you had it?

| m | m | | d | d | | y | y |

Place a photograph of your
bike or skateboard before
its transformation here

Before

Date you finished work

| m | m | d | d | y | y | y | y |

How long did it take to do up?

| m | m | | d | d | | y | y |

How much
did it cost to
do up?   **THINGS TO DO** $

How does the bike/board look now?

Worse ☐   As good ☐   Better ☐   Amazing ☐

Are your friends jealous?   y/n

Place a photograph of your
bike or skateboard after
its transformation here

After

At the same time, you could complete these **Things to Do**
46: Go as Fast as You Can • 55: Invent a New Trend
60: Learn to Live without Something You Love for a Week • 61: Join a Club

Learn to Juggle

The best way to learn how to juggle with three balls is to start with one. Keeping your arms at waist level, start with the ball in your right hand and throw it in an arc to your left hand, to the height of your eye level. [1]. Always keep your eyes focused at this level—if you follow the balls with your eyes, then you're going to make mistakes. Once you've got a feel for this, try using two balls. Hold a ball in each hand. Throw the ball from your right hand to your left. When the ball is at it's highest point (about eye level), throw the other ball in an arc from your left to your right [2]. Try to keep your hands at waist level. If your hands start to wander or you're having to reach to grab wayward balls, then you aren't throwing the balls correctly. Let the ball fall into your hand. DO NOT throw the two balls at the same time.

Ready to juggle with three balls? Hold two balls in your right hand (one in your fingers, the other in the palm) and the third ball in the left [3]. Throw the ball in the fingers of your right hand first, and when it's at its highest point, throw the ball in your left hand [4]. When this ball reaches its greatest height, throw the remaining ball in your right hand [5]. To do this, you'll need to master rolling the third ball to the front of your right hand before you throw it so that the incoming ball can land in the middle of your right hand without interfering with the ball that is about to leave that hand. When you've mastered this, try and juggle by repeating the whole process [6]. ALWAYS keep your eyes focused forward.

Patience and practice: Learning to juggle is a slow process, but as always, practice makes perfect. Do not move on to practicing with two balls until you feel comfortable practicing with one, and so on...

Learn to Juggle **Form**

Once you have completed this **Thing to Do**,
stick your Achieved Star here and fill in the form

☆ Achieved

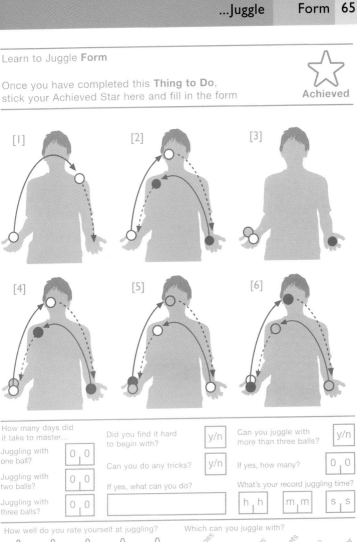

How many days did
it take to master...

Juggling with
one ball? | 0 | 0 |

Juggling with
two balls? | 0 | 0 |

Juggling with
three balls? | 0 | 0 |

Did you find it hard
to begin with? | y/n |

Can you do any tricks? | y/n |

If yes, what can you do?

Can you juggle with
more than three balls? | y/n |

If yes, how many? | 0 | 0 |

What's your record juggling time?
| h | h | | m | m | | s | s |

How well do you rate yourself at juggling?

☆ ☆ ☆ ☆ ☆
Poor   OK   Good   Very good   Excellent

Which can you juggle with?

Oranges □ Pens □ Plates □ Sweets □ Soap □ Other □

At the same time, you could complete these **Things to Do**
7: Prepare Yourself for Fame • 28: Learn to Do a Party Trick
53: Succeed at Something You're Bad At • 61: Join a Club

Have a Snowball Fight and Fun in the Snow

When the snow finally arrives, you've got to make the most of it—especially in parts of the U.S. where it tends to disappear within hours of arriving. So be quick, have fun, and wrap up warm!

Snow Way!

- Snowball fight. It's the first sacred law of snow and a license to attack anyone and everyone—after all, technically it's only water. Pack the snow tightly so that the balls fly faster and longer, but check that there aren't any hard or sharp objects rolled in with it—those could really hurt!
- The second sacred law is build a snowman. Anyone who's young at heart (and not boring) will revel in this simple but deeply satisfying activity. Create a huge snowball with a slightly less huge snowball on top. Voilà! All you need to do then is give your snowman character by adding some facial features and dressing it up. Base it on someone you know, and preferably dislike, because then, after hours of toil on your masterpiece, comes the best bit of all: kicking your snowman into oblivion!
- You don't have to own a fancy toboggan to go sledding. You can use things around the house, e.g., a tin or plastic tray, a thick piece of cardboard, even a trash can liner—although there's no protection when you go over hard snow or stones, so wear at least four pairs of pants!

World's tallest snowman: His name was Angus, King of the Mountain, and he measured 113 ft. 7 in. (34.63 m). He took 14 days to build in February 1999 in the town of Bethel, Maine. Tires were used for his eyes, and instead of twigs for arms, he had trees!

Have a Snowball Fight and Fun in the Snow Form

Once you have completed this **Thing to Do**,
stick your Achieved Star here and fill in the form

Achieved

Snowball fight
Date of your snowball fight

| m | m | d | d | y | y | y | y |

Where were you?

Who did you fight against?

How accurate was
your throwing? | 0 | 0 | 0 | %

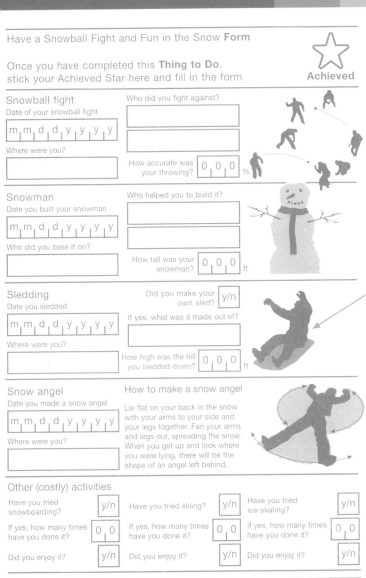

Snowman
Date you built your snowman

| m | m | d | d | y | y | y | y |

Who did you base it on?

Who helped you to build it?

How tall was your
snowman? | 0 | 0 | 0 | ft

Sledding
Date you sledded

| m | m | d | d | y | y | y | y |

Where were you?

Did you make your
own sled? | y/n

If yes, what was it made out of?

How high was the hill
you sledded down? | 0 | 0 | 0 | ft

Snow angel
Date you made a snow angel

| m | m | d | d | y | y | y | y |

Where were you?

How to make a snow angel

Lie flat on your back in the snow
with your arms to your side and
your legs together. Fan your arms
and legs out, spreading the snow.
When you get up and look where
you were lying, there will be the
shape of an angel left behind.

Other (costly) activities

Have you tried
snowboarding? | y/n

If yes, how many times
have you done it? | 0 | 0

Did you enjoy it? | y/n

Have you tried skiing? | y/n

If yes, how many times
have you done it? | 0 | 0

Did you enjoy it? | y/n

Have you tried
ice-skating? | y/n

If yes, how many times
have you done it? | 0 | 0

Did you enjoy it? | y/n

At the same time, you could complete these **Things to Do**
**10: Have an Embarrassing Moment and Get Over It • 29: Climb to the
Top of a Mountain • 46: Go as Fast as You Can • 79: Build an Igloo**

Build the Ultimate Sand Castle and Have Fun in the Sun

Sand, like snow, is one of those things you're never too young or too old to enjoy messing around in. Lying on a beach in the sun is nice for a while, but only boring people can do it all day. Next time you go to the shore, take a bucket and spade. You might feel a bit silly, as the last time you played with them was probably when you were six, but you'll soon wipe the smile off people's faces when they see your amazing sand sculpture.

Mr. Sandman, Bring Me a Dream

- Bring plastic cups, toilet-paper-roll tubes, flowerpots, and anything else that could make a useful mold. The greater range of sizes and shapes the better. Bring tools too, like cutlery, a comb, or a lollipop stick.
- Wet sand is easiest to work with. Mix sand and water thoroughly in your bucket, packing the mixture in really tight. Once the bucket's full, flip it over and tap it on all sides to turn out the sand shape.
- Use your biggest mold first, and build on top of it using smaller ones. This is how you create towers and turrets. If you want to put battlements on, you could use an ice-cube tray as a mold.
- After you've formed a basic castle shape, you can sculpt into it using your tools, forming windows, doors, stairs, gargoyles, and stonework. You can also use shells, seaweed, and bits of wood or plastic to decorate your castle with. Last but not least, dig a moat around the base of your castle and fill it with seawater.

When you've completed your sand castle, you'll need to relax: Get someone to bury you in the sand and have a little snooze. Then when you need freshening up, dash into the waves. Perhaps after that you'll be ready to start some other form of sand sculpture.

Build the Ultimate Sand Castle
and Have Fun in the Sun **Form**
Once you have completed this **Thing to Do**,
stick your Achieved Star here and fill in the form

Achieved

Date you made your sand castle

| m | m | d | d | y | y | y | y |

Where did you build your sand castle?

Did you build it on your own?   y/n

If no, who helped you?

How long did your castle
take to build?   h h   m m

How long did it last?   h h   m m

What destroyed it in the end?

How big was your sand castle?

Height 0 0 in   Width 0 0 in

List the molds you used here

List the tools you used here

How many of these things did your sand castle
feature?

Towers   Windows   Steps   Doors   People   Arches

Was your castle entirely constructed   y/n
of sand and water?

If no, what else did you use?

Shells   Stones   Bits of wood   Junk sculpture   A flag   Other

If other, please specify

Place a photo of your
ultimate sand castle here

At the same time, you could complete these **Things to Do**
1: Send a Message in a Bottle • 32: Visit... • 38: Make a Time Capsule
45: Invent a New Game • 52: Learn to Swim

Take Part in a TV Show

Make your TV-watching experience more interactive by taking part in a show, or get mentioned on the radio and surprise friends who are listening...

Floating on Air

- If one of your favorite TV shows has a studio audience, get on the Internet, find the show or channel's Web site, and see if you can apply for tickets. They're often free, but get them well in advance and arrive at the studio early to make sure you're at the front of the line.
- Write or phone in to take part in a quiz, game, or competition on a radio or TV show. Not only will you get on the air, but you might win a prize too!
- Request a song to be played on a music show and dedicate it to someone you care about. Some TV shows feature on-screen scrolling texts. Text in a message to a friend who's watching, or to the world!
- Some shows have guest presenters or include short films about people with interesting stories to tell. Write in with a suggestion for a feature—starring you! Or write to the producer of a show, saying you're interested in a career in TV and would be grateful for some work experience. That way you might get to take part behind the scenes.
- If someone who bugs you (a politician, perhaps) is on a TV or radio phone-in, think of a question that will really put them on the spot and ask them live on the air. You might also get a chance to speak to your music or film idol this way. You'll need to think of an interesting and original question if you want to be picked from all the other people phoning in.

Get on the news: Let your local radio or TV news know about any exciting or charitable activities you're involved in. One good way to do this is to Lobby Your Local Representative or Get Your School Involved in a World Record Attempt (**Things to Do** Nos. 84 & 11).

Take Part in a TV Show **Form**

Once you have completed this **Thing to Do**,
stick your Achieved Star here and fill in the form

Achieved

Did you take part in a... TV show? ☐ Radio show? ☐

What was the name of the show?

Date you took part

`m m d d y y y y`

Was the show live? `y/n`

How long were you on it for? `s s  m m  h h`

How did you take part?

As an audience member ☐
In a phone-in ☐
In a quiz / game / competition ☐
As a guest presenter ☐
In a news item ☐
Other ☐

If other, please specify

If it was a phone-in, who did you get to talk to?

What was your question?

What was their answer?

If it was a news item, what was it about?

Were you interviewed? `y/n`

If yes, were you pleased with your answers? `y/n`

If it was a game / quiz / competition, what did you have to do?

Did you win? `y/n`

If yes, what did you win?

If you were a presenter, what did you present?

How would you rate your skills as a presenter?

☆ Excellent ☆ Good ☆ OK ☆ Poor ☆ Terrible

Would you like to be a presenter as a job? `y/n`

If you were in the audience, did you get on camera? `y/n`

If yes, what were you doing at the time?

Laughing or smiling ☐
Posing ☐
Picking your nose ☐
Talking to a friend ☐
Looking bored ☐
Other ☐

If other, please specify

How many people you knew saw or heard you? `0 0`

If it was a TV show, did anyone recognize you in the street afterward? `y/n`

At the same time, you could complete these **Things to Do**
7: Prepare Yourself for Fame • 10: Have an Embarrassing Moment
and Get Over It • 18: Win Something • 100: Meet Someone Famous

Would **Hugh Jass** please come to the manager's office...

Make a Scene in a Public Place

William R. Alger, an American writer and minister, once said, "A crowd always thinks with its sympathy, never with its reason." Test this out by seeing how people behave as a group. Call it a science experiment, although really it's a chance to play practical jokes on the unsuspecting general public.

Human Behavioral Experimentation

- Next time you're in a department store with friends, go up to the information desk and tell them you've lost your little brother or sister. Ask them to put out a message over the PA system asking if "Laura Lynn Hardy," "Hugh Jass," "Dinah Soares," or "Duane Pipe" would come to the information desk. See if any shoppers notice.
- Create panic with imaginary animals. Next time you're walking through a park, you could point and scream, "Snake!" Tell the person in front of you on line that they've got a spider crawling up their back.
- Fake a dramatic argument about something wildly imaginative (like stealing a famous boy/girlfriend) with a best friend. Get everyone looking at you as you rant and scream at each other in the middle of the street.
- As you're walking along the street pretend to trip over an invisible wire, and get your friends who are following behind to trip over it too. Look puzzled and walk back to check, tripping over it again. See if any of the people around you try to step over your nonexistent wire!

 Single out people: Shout something at a stranger, like "I love you" or "Give us a kiss" and then hide, leaving your friend standing alone to take the blame. Or if you're feeling braver, greet a stranger in the street to make them think they must know you.

Make a Scene in a Public Place **Form**

Once you have completed this **Thing to Do**,
stick your Achieved Star here and fill in the form

Achieved

PSYCHOLOGICAL PROFILE

—————— SUBJECT: THE GENERAL PUBLIC ——————

Date of experiment

| m | m | d | d | y | y | y | y |

Did you conduct the experiment on
your own? | y/n |

If no, who helped you?

Location in which the experiment took place

Describe the scene before your experiment

Approximate number of
people in the area | 0 | 0 |

Approximate number of people who
reacted to your scene | 0 | 0 |

Were people...

angry? scared? amused? indifferent? shocked? confused? other?

If other, please specify

What was the most common reaction?

What was the most dramatic reaction you got?

How long did it take
people to realize it | h | h | | m | m | | s | s |
was not for real?

Describe the scene after your experiment

Based on your observations, how would you
describe the subject?

sophis-ticated   rational   intelligent   calm   trusting

panicky   gullible   stupid   irrational   insecure

At the same time, you could complete these **Things to Do**
2: Run up an Escalator the Wrong Way • 42: April Fool Someone
54: Be a Daredevil • 88: Blame Someone Else

Spend Christmas in Another Country

The weather can sometimes be a disappointment at Christmas. The snowy scenes you see on the Christmas cards and in the movies may not materialize. So persuade your parents to take you away for a different kind of Christmas.

Snow Good

- Go in search of snow. For the ultimate Christmas winter wonderland, Lapland in Finland is your best bet. Watch out for fat red men with white beards though.
- Go in search of sun. So basking in hot sunshine on Christmas Day might feel a bit odd at first, but the Christmas spirit isn't dependent on cold weather. Ask the Australians! As you're lounging by the pool or on the beach, write postcards to everyone left behind saying, "We're Hot, You're Not."

Snowy Countries at Christmas Time

Norway • Finland • Iceland
Greenland • Switzerland
Russia • Austria • Canada

Hot Countries at Christmas Time

Canary Islands • Australia
South Africa • Thailand
Malaysia • India

Different Christmas Customs

In Finland, the dinner is on Christmas Eve (codfish is traditional), and preceded by a visit to the steam baths. There's no hanging-up of stockings either—Santa comes to visit in person! In France empty shoes are filled instead of stockings. In India banana or mango trees are decorated instead of fir trees. In South Africa lunch is outside and often followed by swimming or a beach trip. Find out how Christmas is celebrated (if at all!) in the country you're going to.

Snow facts: All snowflakes are different, and they always have six sides. The shape of the snowflake is determined by the temperature of the air. The warmer the air, the more spikes and columns they have. In freezing conditions the snow becomes powdery.

Spend Christmas in Another Country **Form**

Once you have completed this **Thing to Do**,
stick your Achieved Star here and fill in the form

☆ **Achieved**

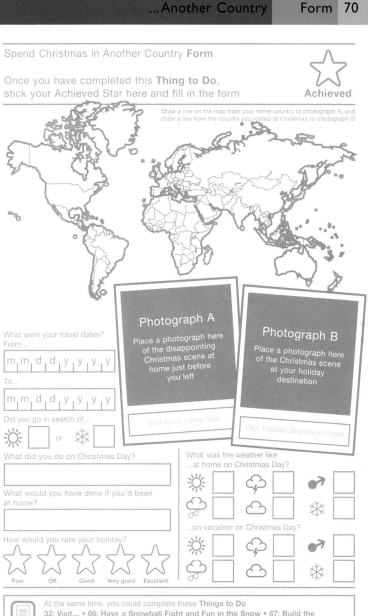

Draw a line on the map from your home country to photograph A, and
draw a line from the country you visited at Christmas to photograph B

Photograph A
Place a photograph here
of the disappointing
Christmas scene at
home just before
you left

Your town name here

Photograph B
Place a photograph here
of the Christmas scene
at your holiday
destination

Your holiday destination here

What were your travel dates?
From...

| m | m | d | d | y | y | y | y |

To...

| m | m | d | d | y | y | y | y |

Did you go in search of...

☀ ☐ or ❄ ☐

What did you do on Christmas Day?

What would you have done if you'd been
at home?

How would you rate your holiday?

☆ ☆ ☆ ☆ ☆
Poor   OK   Good   Very good   Excellent

What was the weather like
...at home on Christmas Day?

☀ ☐   ⛈ ☐   🌬 ☐
🌧 ☐   ☁ ☐   ❄ ☐

...on vacation on Christmas Day?

☀ ☐   ⛈ ☐   🌬 ☐
🌧 ☐   ☁ ☐   ❄ ☐

At the same time, you could complete these **Things to Do**
32: Visit... • 66: Have a Snowball Fight and Fun in the Snow • 67: Build the
Ultimate Sand Castle and Have Fun in the Sun • 97: Learn to Take Great Photos

Do Something Nice without Being Asked

Sometimes when people ask you to do something nice, you feel resentful because they've made you feel guilty for not thinking of doing it yourself— or maybe you thought about it but decided you'd rather watch TV, making you feel even worse! So why not surprise someone by offering to help out of the blue. They'll feel good; you'll feel good. There are no losers.

Do Me a Favor!

- Some people need help more than others. For example, old people, who don't have as much energy as they used to, appreciate any help around the house and garden. If you know someone who's sick, see what you can do for them, or just go over and keep them company. The same goes for anybody who's feeling down. Why not at least buy them chocolates?
- There are plenty of things you can do around the house—your own or your grandparents'—from washing up, to a full-blown spring-cleaning. Washing the car, cleaning windows, and weeding or mowing the lawn are the sorts of jobs that get put off. Why not offer to cook dinner (**Thing to Do** No. 62) or babysit for your parents or your parents' friends?
- Pass on some of your skills. Teach your grandparents how to use the DVD player (**Thing to Do** No. 44). Offer to help a friend study for an exam or a little brother or sister with their homework.
- Help a stranger. If you see a person struggling with something heavy, lend a hand. If someone looks lost, ask if you can help. If you're musical, get down to your local nursing home and offer an hour's entertainment.

That warm feeling you get when you do something nice won't be the reason you do it, although it certainly makes doing it seem more worthwhile. Nor should you do it because you want something in return. However, if you do get paid for your efforts, it's a bonus!

Do Something Nice
without Being Asked **Form**
Once you have completed this **Thing to Do**,
stick your Achieved Star here and fill in the form

Achieved

Date of your good deed

| m | m | d | d | y | y | y | y |

How many nice things have
you done?

| 0 | 0 | 0 |

List the nicest things below

Did you earn any money for your
good deeds?   y/n

THINGS TO DO

If yes, how
much did $
you earn?

Truthfully, did you do nice things just
in case you got paid?   y/n

Do you feel you're a better person
for doing good deeds?   y/n

Has your bout of good deeds
carried on?   y/n

If no, why not?

new level   [3]

parents'   [2]
opinion

usual   [1]
level

GRADING EXAMPLE
On the chart, mark what you think
is your usual level of helpfulness
[1], then ask a parent to grade
you on how helpful you've been
recently [2]. If you disagree with
their grading, add your own
realistic grade [3]. Be truthful!

LEVEL 3
True self-sacrifice,
you saint.

+100

+80

LEVEL 2
You went out of
your way. You've
earned your wings.

+60

+40

LEVEL 1
You've made
a nice gesture.

+20

0

LEVEL 1
You're lazy.

-20

-40

LEVEL 2
You're plain mean.

-60

-80

LEVEL 3
You little devil!

-100

At the same time, you could complete these **Things to Do**
26: Help Save the Planet • 31: Host a Party
33: Learn to Bake a Cake • 43: Do Something Charitable

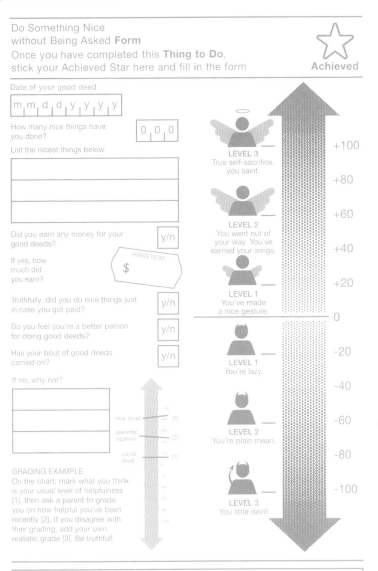

See Your Music Idol Perform Live

Listening to the music you love in your bedroom is one thing, going to hear it being performed live is quite another. You'll be part of an electric atmosphere in a massive room full of other excited fans, listening to the music at impressive new sound levels, and hearing different versions of the songs you love. If you've got every track your music idol's ever put out, the posters, DVDs, books, buttons, key rings, calendars, and T-shirts, then it's definitely time to see them in the flesh.

Sing It Back

- Before the gig, play all your CDs to death, and if they're songs, make sure you learn the words so that you'll be able to sing along.
- When you get there, buy the concert poster or tour T-shirt as a souvenir of your big night out and to keep as proof that you were there. You'll have something to boast about to your friends for days.
- Don't make the classic mistake of thinking the gig's over and leaving before the encore. Clap, whoop, and whistle until your music idol(s) reappears. It may take time, but if they're true professionals who respect their fans, they'll come back for at least one more tune.
- You've been in the same room as your music idol(s), but can you get any closer? It'd be a shame to waste this chance to meet them in person. Hang around outside the stage door after the show to see if you can catch them on their way out. If you do, make sure they sign your T-shirt or program.

 If you go with friends, make T-shirts that spell out a message to your idol and rehearse their moves along to the DVD so you can join in. Wear comfy shoes (you'll be on your feet a lot), but make sure you're stylish, just in case you bump into them after the show.

See Your Music Idol Perform Live **Form**

Once you have completed this **Thing to Do**,
stick your Achieved Star here and fill in the form

Achieved

Date of the concert

m , m , d , d , y , y , y , y

Who did you go with?

Draw your position on the diagram

STAGE

How much did the
ticket cost?

THINGS TO DO

$

Was it worth the money?   y/n

If no, why not?

How good was...
the visual stage show?

☆ ☆ ☆ ☆ ☆
Awesome   Great   OK   Poor   Terrible

the music?

☆ ☆ ☆ ☆ ☆
Awesome   Great   OK   Poor   Terrible

your view?

☆ ☆ ☆ ☆ ☆
Awesome   Great   OK   Poor   Terrible

Did the music sound better live?   y/n

If yes, how did it sound better?

If no, why not?

Did you do any of the following?

Whistle   Pass out   Cheer/
scream   Stamp
your feet   Wave   Dance

Percentage of time   0 , 0   ...and on   0 , 0
you spent sat down.   your feet

Did your music idol play an encore?   y/n

If yes, how many encores did they do?   0 , 0

And how many songs did they play in
total?   0 , 0

What souvenirs did you take home with you?

Did you get to meet your music idol in
person?   y/n

If yes, how?

Who would you like to see perform next?

At the same time, you could complete these **Things to Do**
32: Visit... • 61: Join a Club • 68: Take Part in a TV Show
86: Sing in Front of an Audience • 100: Meet Someone Famous

Have a Sleepover

A good day doesn't have to stop at bedtime, not if you've got all your friends over for the night. Sleepovers are a great way to bond—a few secrets are bound to slip out during the course of the evening. See how late you can keep the fun going, but try not to argue with any of your friends, as you'll have to put up with them all night. Everyone needs to bring a pillow, sleeping bag, pair of pajamas and toothbrush, and you're ready to party.

A Hard Day's Night

- Get ready for bed good and early so that when you finally start to tire out late at night (or early in the morning), all you have to do is collapse into your sleeping bag without the hassle of getting ready for bed.
- Set up camp in the living room, where there's lots of entertainment and more space. Make sure your family has everything they need from there before you get started so they don't have an excuse to interrupt.
- Start with some food, like pizzas or hot dogs. Make sure you have a supply of snacks and drinks too for your midnight feast (or breakfast!).
- Good ways to spend the early part of the evening are computer-game tournaments, card games, makeovers, truth or dare, charades, and, of course, the essential pillow fight! Later, when you need to keep the noise down, move on to films. Watch a scary one, and then tell each other ghost stories in the dark. It's probably best to watch a comedy afterward though. You don't want to be kept up with nightmares.

Sleeping-bag fun: Ask someone to leave the room. While they're outside everyone swaps sleeping bags and hides inside. When the person returns, they have to guess who's in each bag by getting the people inside to make noises that give their identity away.

Have a Sleepover Form

Once you have completed this **Thing to Do**,
stick your Achieved Star here and fill in the form

Achieved

Date of the sleepover

m m d d y y y y

How many people came
to your sleepover? 0 0

What time did it start? : PM

What time did you get
to sleep? : PM
AM

What did you eat?

Did you...

Have a
pillow fight?
Watch
films?
Play computer
games?
Make each
other over?
Tell
secrets?

Play Truth
or Dare?
Play card
games?
Play
Charades?
Tell ghost
stories?
Eat too
much?

Did you get told off for
anything? y/n

If yes, what did you get told off for?

Who fell asleep first?

Whose turn is it next to have a sleepover?

What did you get up to? Write your itinerary here

6PM

7PM

8PM

9PM

10PM

11PM

12PM

1AM

2AM

Place a photo of you and
all the guests at your
sleepover here

At the same time, you could complete these **Things to Do**
9: Play a Computer Game to the End • 20: Stay Up All Night • 21: Sleep All Day
31: Host a Party • 56: Know Who Your Friends Are • 83: Dye Your Hair

SPY**CORP**

UNDERCOVER
& OVERRATED

Cover name:

ID No: 02 7892 007 27___

Age:

Signature:

Place your photo here

Become a Spy

The secret to becoming a successful spy is having nerves of steel; top skills in acting, stealth, persuasion, and secrecy; and lots of patience. Once you've learned how to get the information you want, turn it to your advantage. But first you need to develop a secret identity, so choose a cover name and make a fake ID. Then use the missions below as part of your spy training.

Mission Objectives

- **Mission One:** Assume your new identity, get a disguise, and go under-cover. Fool people you know into thinking you're someone you're not.
- **Mission Two:** Talk your way out of a tricky situation.
- **Mission Three:** Extract information you need from someone without them realizing what you're doing by using your skills of persuasion.
- **Mission Four:** Make it in and out of the kitchen from your room without being discovered. Return with a snack. Do a recce (recon-naissance) before you go so you know what the security situation is.
- **Mission Five:** When you're out with friends, lose them in a crowd and then tail them from a safe distance. Don't let them spot you. Don't let them out of your sight. Take photos of them with your spy phone.
- **Soyyout Yod:** Zxe zu mgot giikyy zu euax yoyzkx, hxuznkx ux g lxoktj'y xuus gtj zgqk vnuzumxgvny ul znkox vxobgzk yzall. Yktj znk vnuzuy hgiq zu znks ot znk vuyz.*

---

*To decipher **Mission Six**, you'll need to turn to **Thing to Do** No. 22 (Invent a Secret Code) and work out which of the codes on those pages (if you examine them closely, two are given) have been used here. Decode the mission and complete it.

Become a Spy **Form**

Once you have completed this **Thing to Do**,
stick your Achieved Star here and fill in the form

Achieved

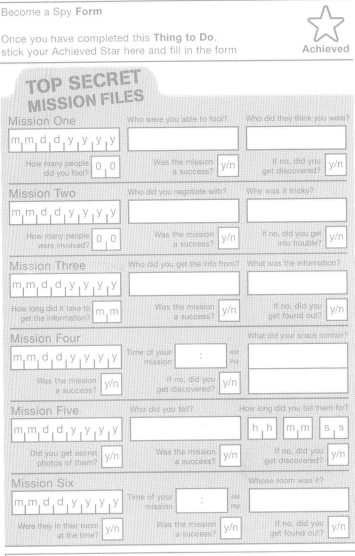

TOP SECRET MISSION FILES

Mission One

m m d d y y y y

How many people did you fool? | 0 0

Who were you able to fool?

Who did they think you were?

Was the mission a success? y/n

If no, did you get discovered? y/n

Mission Two

m m d d y y y y

How many people were involved? | 0 0

Who did you negotiate with?

Why was it tricky?

Was the mission a success? y/n

If no, did you get into trouble? y/n

Mission Three

m m d d y y y y

How long did it take to get the information? m m

Who did you get the info from?

What was the information?

Was the mission a success? y/n

If no, did you get found out? y/n

Mission Four

m m d d y y y y

Time of your mission : AM PM

What did your snack contain?

Was the mission a success? y/n

If no, did you get discovered? y/n

Mission Five

m m d d y y y y

Who did you tail?

How long did you tail them for?

h h m m s s

Did you get secret photos of them? y/n

Was the mission a success? y/n

If no, did you get discovered? y/n

Mission Six

m m d d y y y y

Time of your mission : AM PM

Whose room was it?

Were they in their room at the time? y/n

Was the mission a success? y/n

If no, did you get found out? y/n

At the same time, you could complete these **Things to Do**
22: Invent a Secret Code • 27: Turn Back Time
80: Start Your Own Secret Society

Watch a Tadpole Grow into a Frog

If you've grown a plant from a seed (**Thing to Do** No. 57), then it's time to watch another of nature's babies grow up. Frog metamorphosis is incredible—it allows an underwater creature to transform into one that can live on land too. Over a few months you can see a tadpole change into a froglet, and then hopefully, if it hasn't hopped off already, a fully developed frog.

Toadily Awesome!

- Find a pond you can visit regularly. It could be in a garden, out in the country, or in a park—if the area around the pond is damp and cool, there's a good chance that some frogs will come there to breed.
- The best time to find frog spawn is February and March. Look in the shallow parts of the pond, where frogs tend to lay their eggs. The eggs are protected in a clear, jellylike substance, and one frog can lay thousands; so if they're there, they shouldn't be too hard to find!
- Depending on the temperature, it can take from several days up to a few weeks for the eggs to develop into tadpoles (cold weather will slow things down). You'll be able to see them taking shape through the jelly-like substance. After about a month the tadpoles will start to hatch.
- Now comes the exciting bit—watching them develop into frogs. This takes about three months. Use the chart opposite to monitor their progress. Remember throughout the process to look, but don't touch!

Frogs or toads? Frogs lay their eggs in clusters, whereas toads lay them in chains and their tadpoles tend to be smaller and darker than a frog's. Also, when fully grown, frogs are slimy and smooth, and toads are warty and dry.

Watch a Tadpole Grow into a Frog **Form**

Once you have completed this **Thing to Do**,
stick your Achieved Star here and fill in the form

Achieved

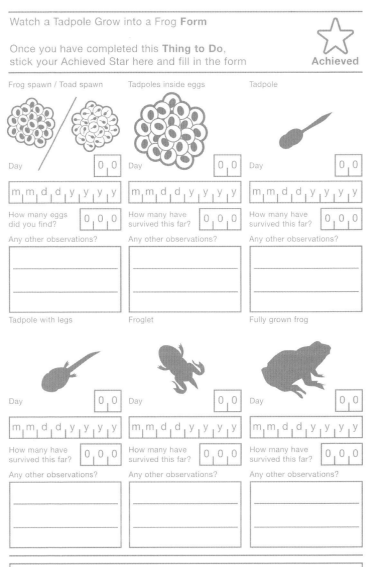

Frog spawn / Toad spawn

Day `0 0`

`m m d d y y y y`

How many eggs `0 0 0`
did you find?

Any other observations?

Tadpoles inside eggs

Day `0 0`

`m m d d y y y y`

How many have `0 0 0`
survived this far?

Any other observations?

Tadpole

Day `0 0`

`m m d d y y y y`

How many have `0 0 0`
survived this far?

Any other observations?

Tadpole with legs

Day `0 0`

`m m d d y y y y`

How many have `0 0 0`
survived this far?

Any other observations?

Froglet

Day `0 0`

`m m d d y y y y`

How many have `0 0 0`
survived this far?

Any other observations?

Fully grown frog

Day `0 0`

`m m d d y y y y`

How many have `0 0 0`
survived this far?

Any other observations?

At the same time, you could complete these **Things to Do**
26: Help Save the Planet • 32: Visit... • 40: Take Care of an Animal
52: Learn to Swim • 92 Have Your Own Plot in the Garden

Learn to Say Useful Phrases in Other Languages

There are around 6,700 languages in the world, spoken in over 200 countries. Unless you were lucky enough to be brought up bilingually, you can probably only speak one of those languages fluently, and maybe a little of one or two others. Having English as a first language is a real bonus, as it's such an international language. However, when you're abroad, don't expect everyone to speak your language. You need to show that you're interested in their language and culture. They'll appreciate any effort you make.

Learn the Lingo

Here are some key phrases you should know. Remember that there's no point in learning a question if you've no hope of understanding the answer:

- "Do you speak English?" It's easy to forget what you've learned when you're on the spot, and some things are just too difficult to say. Have this question ready just in case, and cross your fingers that the answer's yes.
- "Where's the bathroom?" Essential information. You're an ambassador for your nation. You don't want to get caught short in another country.
- "Will you e-mail me when I'm gone?" or "Can I have your e-mail address?" You never know when you're going to make a new friend or have a holiday romance. It's important to know when you leave if your new friendship is going to last. Be direct and ask.
- "They're not with me." Your family will embarrass you plenty of times on vacation. Make sure people know that they have nothing to do with you.
- "Are you sure this is edible?" For food you don't like the look of.

Talk in pictures: If your cell has a camera on it, take pictures of things you might need to ask or talk about (e.g., the bathroom, your hotel, your family, a beach or swimming pool, a station, train or bus), and use them as visual aids if you get stuck with the language.

Learn to Say Useful Phrases in Other Languages **Form**

Once you have completed this **Thing to Do**,
stick your Achieved Star here and fill in the form

★ **Achieved**

Learn essential phrases in five other languages

ENGLISH	FRENCH	SPANISH	GERMAN	ITALIAN	CHINESE
Do you speak English?	Parlez-vous anglais?	¿Hablas inglés?	Sprechen Sie Englisch?	Parla inglese?	ni hui shuo ying yu ma?
Where's the toilet?	Où sont les toilettes?	¿Dónde están los lavabos?	Wo sind die Toiletten?	Dov'è il bagno?	ce suo zai na er?
Can I have your e-mail address?	Quel est ton adresse d'email?	¿Me das tu dirección de correo electrónico?	Was ist deine Adresse?	Mi dai il tuo e-mail?	neng gao su wo ni de email di zhi ma?
They're not with me!	Je ne les connais pas!	No estoy con ellos.	Ich kenne sie nicht!	Non sono con me!	ta men bu shi he wo yi qi de!
Are you sure this is edible?	C'est comestible?	¿Seguro que se puede comer esto?	Kann ich das wirklich essen?	Sei certo(a) é commestibile?	ni que ding zhe ge neng chi ma?
Hello/Goodbye	Bonjour/Au revoir	Hola/Adiós	Guten Tag/Auf Wiedersehen	Buongiorno/Arrivederci (or Ciao for both)	ni hao/zai jian
Please/Thank you	S'il vous plaît/Merci	Por favor/Gracias	Bitte/Danke	Per favore/Grazie	qing/xie xie
How much is it?	C'est combien?	¿Cuanto cuesta esto?	Wieviel kostet das?	Quanto costa?	zhe ge duo shao qian?
one, two, three, four, five, six, seven, eight, nine, ten	un, deux, trois, quatre, cinq, six, sept, huit, neuf, dix	uno, dos, tres, cuatro, cinco, seis, siete, ocho, nueve, diez	eins, zwei, drei, vier, fünf, sechs, sieben, acht, neun, zehn	uno, due, tre, quattro, cinque, sei, sette, otto, nove, dieci	yi, er, san, si, wu, liu, qi, ba, jiu, shi
I like.	J'aime.	Me gusta(n).	Ich mag...	Mi piace...	wo xi huan...
I don't like...	Je n'aime pas...	No me gusta(n)...	Ich mag nicht...	Non mi piace...	wo bu xi huan...
I understand	Je comprends	Entiendo	Ich verstehe	Capisco	wo li jie
I don't understand	Je ne comprends pas	No entiendo	Ich verstehe nicht	Non capisco	wo bu li jie
I would like...	Je voudrais...	Me gustaria ...	Ich möchte...	Vorrei...	wo xiang yao...
What is it?	Qu'est-ce que c'est?	¿Qué es?	Was ist das?	Che cos'è?	zhe shi shen me?
I don't eat...	Je ne mange pas...	No como...	Ich esse kein/keine	Non mangio...	wo bu chi...
Big/Little	Grande/Petit(e)	Grande/Pequeño	Gross/Klein	Grande/Piccolo	da/xiao
What's your name?	Comment vous appelez-vous?	¿Cómo te llamas?	Wie heisst du?	Come ti chiami?	ni jiao shen me ming zi?
My name is...	Je m'appelle...	Me llamo...	Ich heisse...	Mi chiamo...	wo jiao...
How old are you?	Quel âge avez-vous?	¿Cuantos años tienes?	Wie alt bist du?	Quanti anni hai?	ni duo da le?
Do you have a boyfriend/girlfriend?	Vous avez un copain/ une copine?	¿Tienes novio/novia?	Hast du ein Freund/ eine Freundin?	Hai un ragazzo/ una ragazza?	ni you nan/nu peng you ma?
Where is...?	Où est...?	¿Dónde esta...?	Wo ist die/der/das...	Dov'e...?	...zai na er?
How do I get to...?	Pour aller au/a la ... s'il vous plaît?	¿Cómo llegaria a ...?	Wie komme ich am besten zum/zur...	Come ci si arriva...?	wo zen me qu...?
I'm lost. Can you help me?	Je suis perdue(e). Pouvez-vous m'aider?	Me he perdido. ¡Ayúdame!	Ich bin hier fremd. Koennten Sie mir helfen?	Mi sono smarrito(a). Aiuto!	wo mi lu le. jiu ming!
Left/Right/Straight on	À gauche/A droite/ Tout droit	Izquierda/Derecha/ Todo recto	Links/Rechts/Geradeaus	Sinistra/Destra/Sempre dritto	zuo/you/zhi zou

At the same time, you could complete these **Things to Do**
32: Visit... • 35: Learn How to Ask Someone Out (and How to Dump Them)
70: Spend Christmas in Another Country • 97: Learn to Take Great Photos

Make Your Own Greeting Cards

The best way to wish someone a Happy Birthday, Merry Christmas, or to Get Well Soon is to give them a homemade card. People really appreciate cards that have been made rather than bought, so get your pens, pencils, old magazines, photos, and glue out, and get busy!

Greetings!

- It's important to choose the right subject matter for your card. Think about what the person receiving the card is into and illustrate it. If it's football, show them playing with their favorite team. If they like music or film, why not picture them on the stage or set with their idol—or even being them!
- Make your card funny. If it makes the person you're giving it to laugh, then they'll show it to everyone and it'll be the only card they keep long after their birthday, illness, or Christmas has passed.
- You don't have to be artistic to make a greeting card. Cut out the head of the person it's for from an old photo, and paste it to the body of someone famous, onto an animal, or into a scene where they don't belong. Add a caption or something funny in a speech bubble.
- At Christmas you may not have time to make individual cards for everyone, so why not make your designs on a computer, or if you have access to a computer with a scanner, scan your design into the computer? This way you can print off lots of copies.

The greeting card industry started to take off back in the 1840s when stamps were introduced into the postal system. Before then, only well-off people could afford to commission artists to engrave and print cards and get them hand-delivered.

Make Your Own Greeting Cards **Form**

Once you have completed this **Thing to Do**,
stick your Achieved Star here and fill in the form

Achieved

Use the template below to make your cards, or visit the Web site for a template

BIRTHDAY/CHRISTMAS

MOTHER'S/FATHER'S DAY

HAPPY

MERRY

The message in
this card reads:

ABCDEFGHIJKLM
NOPQRSTUVWXY
Z ($¢&.*,?!)

I LOVE YOU MORE / THAN LIFE ITSELF / THAN THE TV

1234567890

At the same time, you could complete these **Things to Do**
33: Learn to Bake a Cake • 35: Learn How to Ask Someone Out (and How to Dump
Them) • 71: Do Something Nice without Being Asked • 91: Send a Valentine Card

Hold a Garage Sale

It's easy to hang on to things in case they might be useful, or perhaps you just forget about them and move on to something new. But clutter builds up without you even realizing and pretty soon you've got boxes and boxes of stuff that is either broken, you don't use, or you didn't like in the first place, like all those Christmas and birthday presents that you were given and didn't play with again. But combine your junk with the whole family's and you'll have plenty of stuff to sell.

Buy, Buy, Sell, Sell!

- Be prepared to haggle. Make the price low enough to get people interested but high enough to give the buyer a chance to haggle. (For instance, if you think an item is worth $1, price it at $2. If you get haggled down to $1, you haven't lost anything; BUT if they buy it for $2 you've made twice as much as you were expecting!)
- Hold it on a day when good weather is forecast, or no one will turn up.
- Hold it in your garage or front yard. If you don't live on a busy street, make some posters and put them up a couple of days beforehand in a local convenience store's windows and on lampposts. If you have lots of great stuff, it may be better to ask someone to take you and your junk to a flea market. You may have to pay for a plot to sell from, but it shouldn't be very much, and you're pretty much guaranteed a big crowd.
- If you're still left with lots of items you want rid of, sell them on eBay.*

---

 * eBay is the world's largest garage sale: It's a place where you can buy and sell pretty much anything you like and there are millions of shoppers. It works like an auction, so you don't choose what price to sell things at; buyers will bid for them and the highest bid wins.

Hold a Garage Sale **Form**

Once you have completed this **Thing to Do**,
stick your Achieved Star here and fill in the form

Achieved

Date of your garage sale

m , m , d , d , y , y , y , y

Who helped you with the sale?

Did you advertise the sale?   y/n

Time of your garage sale

:   –   :

Where did you hold the sale?

Did the weather hold out for you?   y/n

Draw over the pie chart example below, and enter the % of items that were yours and the % of items that were other people's

Draw over the pie chart example below and enter the % of items sold that were yours and the % of items sold that were other people's

Things-to-Sell Pie Chart

Your stuff

Brother's/ sister's stuff

Parent's stuff

Other people's stuff

Things-Sold Pie Chart

Didn't sell

Your stuff

Parent's stuff

Brother's/ sister's stuff

Other people's stuff

Was the garage sale a success?   y/n

What was the silliest item you sold?

How much did it sell for?   THINGS TO DO $

What was the most expensive item you sold?

How much did it sell for?   THINGS TO DO $

Approximately how many people came to your garage sale?   0 , 0 , 0

How many items were you left with?   0 , 0 , 0

What didn't sell?

How much money did you make?   THINGS TO DO $

What have you done with the money?

At the same time, you could complete these **Things to Do**
25: Start a Collection • 43: Do Something Charitable
51: Save Your Pocket Money for a Month and Spend It All at Once

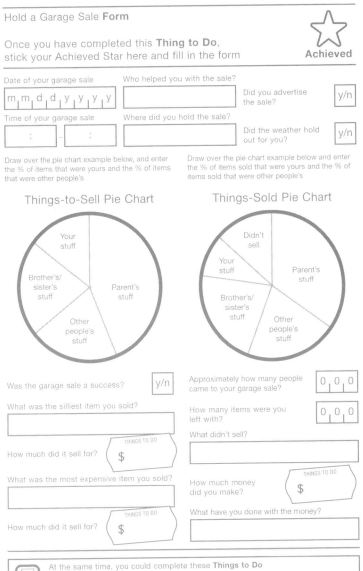

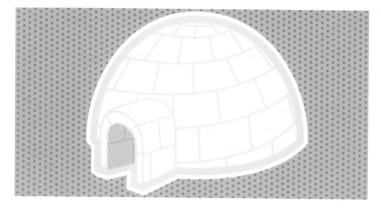

Build an Igloo

This is a real challenge and one that requires plenty of warm clothes and strong teamwork, so bring a helper. All you need is a spade and a saw. Oh yes, and LOTS of snow.

Bricking It

- Make sure the snow is hard and deep enough to make blocks out of. If it isn't compacted, the blocks will crumble in your hand. Try packing the snow down underfoot if it's a bit powdery. Mark a circle on the ground big enough to fit two to three people lying down comfortably.
- The blocks should be about 32 in (80 cm) long, 8 in (20 cm) deep and 20 in (50 cm) at their highest [1]. The first one will be about 10 in (25 cm) high though, as you need to make the blocks spiral upward rather than place them flat to the floor. So the height of each block will increase as you work around the circle [2].
- After the first level, make sure the blocks are beveled (cut at an angle) to slant inward toward the center of the igloo. Your friend will need to stand on the inside to help adjust the blocks for a snug fit and stop them from falling over. As you work up, the blocks need to become smaller and more angled at each level so that the igloo can form a dome [3].
- When you get to the top (about shoulder level) you'll be left with a hole to fill with a single block. The dome is now complete, but your helper will be trapped inside! At the side of the igloo (away from the wind), dig down under the igloo wall and up into the main part of the igloo [4]. Finally you must cut air vents into the side of your igloo!

Helpful tips: Cut and smooth the blocks near to your igloo so you don't have to travel far with them. Once in place, you can do further shaping as necessary (getting them to slope up). Cut the last block a bit larger than the top hole, so you can shape it from below to fit.

Build an Igloo **Form**

Once you have completed this **Thing to Do**,
stick your Achieved Star here and fill in the form

Achieved

Date you built an igloo

| m | m | d | d | y | y | y | y |

Where were you?

Who helped you?

How long did it
take to build? | h | h | | m | m |

Did the igloo go according to plan? | y/n |

If no, what happened?

Place a photograph of you
and your finished igloo here

How to build an igloo

[1]

[2]

[3]

[4]

At the same time, you could complete these **Things to Do**
29: Climb to the Top of a Mountain • 59: Camp Out in the Backyard
66: Have a Snowball Fight and Fun in the Snow

Start Your Own Secret Society

Now you've learned how to be a spy (**Thing to Do** No. 73) and you've invented your secret code (**Thing to Do** No. 22), it's time to start your own secret society and put all those skills to good use.

Strictly Hush-Hush

- Figure out what you'd like your secret society for. Is it ghost hunting? Antibullying? Detective work? Or general mischief? Once you've decided what the aim of your society is, invite like-minded friends to join. Then you should discuss the details of how you will operate and what kind of missions you'll take on.
- The whole point of the society is that it must operate secretly. Its existence MUST be kept to members only. If someone blabs about it to nonmembers, that person should be expelled.
- Other things you'll need to decide upon are:
  - The name of your secret society. Think of something that can be abbreviated, e.g., S.N.O.O.P. (Secret Network of Outstanding People)
  - Who is (and isn't) allowed to join the society.
  - How often and where you're going to meet. (Find a secret den.)
  - A motto and rules for members of the society. You could also invent a secret handshake and a secret code to use for safe communication.
  - A club logo. Design a sign/symbol that will only be recognized by society members, and use it to make buttons or T-shirts.

Club members: Only invite a couple of your most trustworthy friends to join the secret society at the start. You could set up a system whereby members can nominate people to join, but the whole group must agree before inviting anyone new.

Start Your Own Secret Society **Form**

Once you have completed this **Thing to Do**,
stick your Achieved Star here and fill in the form

Achieved

Secret Society Policy

I, (your name here), invite you, the undersigned, into my secret society.
The name of the society shall be (society name here). The purpose of the
society shall be as follows:

Secret society rules: Do not talk about the secret society. Talking about it
will result in expulsion from the society. Entry to the secret society is by
nomination only. Other rules include:

The secret society will meet every (write when here).
Missing the meeting twice in a row could result in
expulsion

Founding members of the secret society to sign here

DO NOT
talk about the
secret society

At the same time, you could complete these **Things to Do**
19: Make a T-shirt • 22: Invent a Secret Code • 47: Make Your Own Buttons
56: Know Who Your Friends Are • 74: Become a Spy

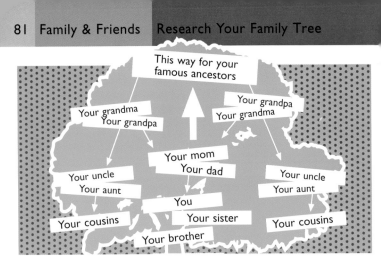

This way for your famous ancestors

Your grandma
Your grandpa

Your grandpa
Your grandma

Your mom
Your dad

Your uncle
Your aunt

Your uncle
Your aunt

You

Your cousins

Your sister
Your brother

Your cousins

Research Your Family Tree

Like it or not, we are who we are because of who we're related to: it's in the genes. So why not find out about your ancestors? You might discover more about yourself. You could turn out to be related to someone famous, maybe even a long-lost member of the royal family!

We Are Family

- Don't be too ambitious to start with. It's hard to find out about people who died a very long time ago, and family trees can get pretty complicated rather quickly. Check if anyone else in the family ever started a tree. Otherwise, aim to go back five generations (to your grandparents' grandparents), concentrating your efforts on family related to you by blood, and starting with one side (e.g., your mom's) before moving across to the other. Any further back than that will be a bonus.

- Start by quizzing your living relatives, especially parents and grandparents. They can tell you about their parents and grandparents, and will hopefully own letters, documents, and photos to help you build a clearer picture. You can probably trace your family back to the 1800s just by talking to the relatives you have!

- There are official documents which may help your research. The National Archives will tell you what information is available and how to get hold of it (see the box below). Help is also available if you have family members who come from abroad.

---

www.archives.gov/genealogy will direct you to helpful research tools, like birth, death, and marriage certificates and census records.

Research Your Family Tree **Form**

Once you have completed this **Thing to Do**,
stick your Achieved Star here and fill in the form

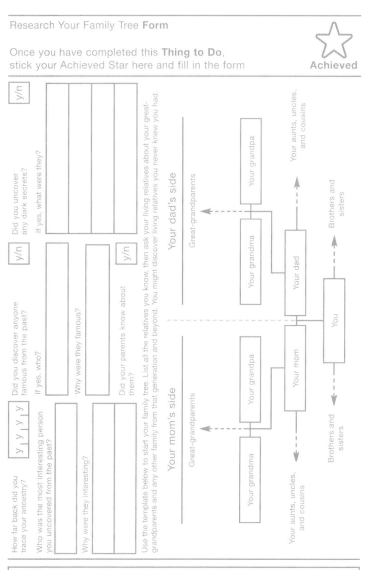

Achieved

Did you uncover any dark secrets? y/n
If yes, what were they?

Did you discover anyone famous from the past? y/n
If yes, who?
Why were they famous?

Did your parents know about them? y/n

How far back did you trace your ancestry? y_y_y_y

Who was the most interesting person you uncovered from the past?

Why were they interesting?

Use the template below to start your family tree. List all the relatives you know, then ask your living relatives about your great-grandparents and any other family from that generation and beyond. You might discover living relatives you never knew you had.

Your dad's side

Great-grandparents

Your grandpa

Your grandma

Your aunts, uncles, and cousins

Your dad

Brothers and sisters

You

Your mom's side

Great-grandparents

Your grandpa

Your grandma

Your mom

Your aunts, uncles, and cousins

Brothers and sisters

At the same time, you could complete these **Things to Do**
44: Teach Your Grandparents Something New
101: Decide What You Want to Be When You Grow Up

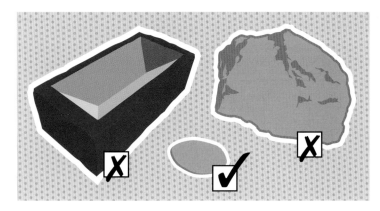

Learn to Skip Stones

It's great fun, it doesn't cost any money, and all you need is a stone or two and a lot of water. Beware, though, it may take patience and a bit of practice, but once you start skipping stones, it's very hard to stop.

Skippy-Dipping

- The most important thing is to find a stone that is likely to skip across the surface of the water—the flatter and smoother, the better. It's often easy to find oval stones on the beach or shore of a lake, as this is the shape that constant rubbing of the water wears them into, but triangular flat stones skip best.
- For the best results the water has to be as calm as possible. Waves will disturb the surface of the water and prevent your stone from bouncing.
- When throwing your stone, get as low as possible to the water, as height will take the speed out of your stone much quicker. Try and throw your stone from about ankle height. The secret to throwing the stone is to add spin; so when you throw your stone, flick your wrist as you let go of it. Speed is more desirable than strength.
- Once your stone is released, it should skip across the surface of the water. This is caused by the resistance between the stone and the surface tension of the water. Every time the stone touches the surface, it will leave behind it a trail of rippled water. Measure your success by how far your stone skips, or by how many times it hits the water.

Skipping-stones world record: So far, the record for the most times a stone has skipped across the surface of water is 38 times. This record is held by Jerdone Coleman-McGhee and was accomplished on the Blanco River in Texas in 1994.

Learn to Skip Stones **Form**

Once you have completed this **Thing to Do**,
stick your Achieved Star here and fill in the form

Achieved

Tick the box for each time you managed to make the stone skip. Try and break the current record of 38 times, but be warned! It's not as easy as it looks!

1	2	3
4	5	6	7
8	9	10	11
12	13	14	15
16	17	18	19
20	21	22	23
24	25	26	27
28	29	30	31
32	33	34	35
36	37	38	39

Current world record   New world record!

At the same time, you could complete these **Things to Do**
1: Send a Message in a Bottle • 32: Visit...
45: Invent a New Game • 52: Learn to Swim

Dye Your Hair

It's surprising the difference the way you wear your hair makes to the way you look overall. Dying hair is a surefire way to shock people, as it's a sudden and sometimes dramatic change. Parents may disapprove, but really, what's the harm? It washes out, and as long as you follow the instructions correctly (read them twice!), it should be quite safe. It's your hair, so let it be on your head to accept the consequences of your actions!

Dying to See You

- You can get fantastic colors fairly cheaply that are easy to use and semi-permanent (i.e., they wash out—check first how long they take). Always go to a professional hairdresser for permanent changes (e.g., bleaching).
- You'll need rubber gloves to protect your hands (usually supplied with the dye), a comb to distribute the dye evenly through your hair, old clothes, an old towel, and a watch to time how long the dye stays in.
- Do a strand or skin test (whatever the instructions recommend) before using the dye on your hair. You don't want to discover too late that your hair has gone green instead of pink, or that you're allergic to the dye.
- Dying is a messy business (hence the old clothes and towel). Have a wet cloth on hand to wipe away drips immediately, and wrap your hair up in a plastic bag while you're waiting for it to take in the dye.
- Double-check how long the dye is supposed to stay in, and when the time is up, wash your hair thoroughly to remove any residue.
- Now go downstairs and scare the pants off your parents.

Pick a color to complement your skin tones: Don't choose reds if you have a reddish complexion. If you're very pale, be aware that dark colors like black will emphasize this. You could end up looking rather ill. But then, maybe that's the look you're after!

Dye Your Hair **Form**

Once you have completed this **Thing to Do**,
stick your Achieved Star here and fill in the form

Achieved

What color did you dye your
hair? Color in the diagram
with the exact color or
place a photo here

Date you dyed your hair

m	m	d	d	y	y	y	y

What is your natural color?

What color did you dye it?

How long did the color last?

m	m		w	w		d	d

Did you dye it
on your own?   y/n

If no, who helped you?

Did you make a mess?   y/n

How happy are you with the result?

☆ Very   ☆ Quite   ☆ It's OK   ☆ Not very   ☆ I hate it!

What was your parents' reaction?

Positive Negative Complementary Shock Fury Other

☐ ☐ ☐ ☐ ☐ ☐

If other, please specify

Did you get into trouble for
dying your hair?   y/n

If yes, did you have to dye it
back to your natural color?   y/n

Do your friends think you look cool?   y/n

Has anyone copied you?   y/n

If yes, who?

What other colors would you like to try?

At the same time, you could complete these **Things to Do**
**10: Have an Embarrassing Moment and Get Over It • 54: Be a Daredevil
55: Invent a New Trend • 74: Become a Spy**

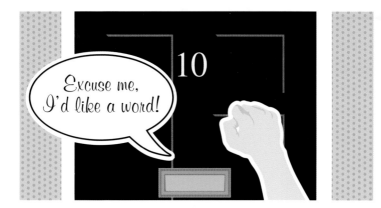

Lobby Your Local Representative

You might be too young to vote, but that doesn't mean you should sit back and let the adults run the country without having your say in how things should be done. Representatives take up issues that people living in their constituency (the people they represent) care about, and they are used to getting letters from people who are worried about an issue or a good cause. Representatives can talk to other people in power…and hopefully get some results.

Make Your Voice Heard

- Find out the name of your representative. If none of your friends, family or teachers knows, type "Find my representative" into a search engine on the Internet. You can write to them at House of Representatives, Washington, D.C.
- What do you want to write to your representative about? Is it a local issue, such as a community baseball field being turned into an apartment complex? Or is it a global concern, like the emission of greenhouse gases? Watch the news and read your local papers to keep up with events that affect you. Send a letter stating your concerns, what action you'd like your representative to take, and request a reply. Hopefully, they'll take action on your behalf.
- You'll probably receive a polite letter or postcard in response with the House of Representatives seal on it. Depending on their reply, you might need to write back and get into a real correspondence. Who knows, you may get so interested in politics that you decide you want to be a representative yourself—or even president (**Thing to Do** No. 101).

 Campaigner: Do you know people who feel the same way as you? Then start a petition and encourage them to write to their representative too. Check out this government fact sheet for more information about contacting representatives: www.house.gov/writerep

Lobby Your Local MP **Form**

Once you have completed this **Thing to Do**,
stick your Achieved Star here and fill in the form

Achieved

Name of your representative

Briefly describe what your letter was about

Date you wrote your representative a letter

m | m | d | d | y | y | y | y

Did you write to them about…

a local issue? [ ]   a global concern? [ ]

Did you include a petition? [y/n]

If yes, how many
signatures did you get? [0 | 0 | 0 | 0 | 0 | 0]

Write your representative's response below

HOUSE OF REPRESENTATIVES
WASHINGTON, D.C., 20515

m | m | d | d | y | y | y | y

Dear (your name here)

Was it a quick response? [y/n]

What is your next plan of action?

How would you rate your representative's response?

☆ ☆ ☆ ☆ ☆
Positive Promising Not sure Unhelpful Pathetic

At the same time, you could complete these **Things to Do**
26: Help Save the Planet • 93: Build Your Own Web site
101: Decide What You Want to Be When You Grow Up

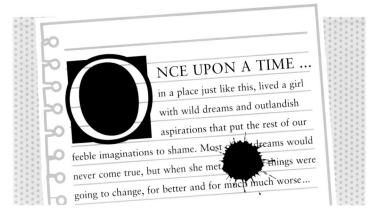

ONCE UPON A TIME ...

in a place just like this, lived a girl with wild dreams and outlandish aspirations that put the rest of our feeble imaginations to shame. Most of our dreams would never come true, but when she met ▉▉▉ things were going to change, for better and for much much worse...

Write a Story and Get It Published

Writing a good story can be hard work. Sometimes it helps to work out the plot before you actually start writing. But it can also be fun to come up with a great idea for the opening, and then just keep going and see what happens. Either way, you'll need a great idea to get you started.

Once Upon a Time...

- Inspiration can come anytime and anywhere—keep your eyes and ears open! J. K. Rowling famously came up with the idea for Harry Potter on the train. You might get inspired on the way to school, visiting a museum, or gazing out of the window during a math lesson! Make sure you write down your idea before you forget it.
- Look back at your own experiences for more inspiration. You could incorporate some of the sadder or funnier things that have happened to you into the lives of your characters.
- Show your story to people whose opinions you respect and get some feedback. Don't be put off if not everything they say is good. You can always go back and change things if you agree with their comments.
- When you're happy with your story, look in newspapers, magazines, and on the Internet for competitions to enter. Winning entries are bound to be published. You could also send it in to literary magazines in the hope one of them likes it and decides to publish it. Definitely submit it to your school magazine, if you have one.

 If you can't get your story published, at least print copies for your family and friends. You could even add your own illustrations and bind the finished product nicely in a folder. Leave a copy for a stranger on the train. Let the world see your work!

Write a Story and Get It Published **Form**

Once you have completed this **Thing to Do**,
stick your Achieved Star here and fill in the form

Achieved

Did you get your story published? y/n

If no, did you decide to "publish" it yourself?

If yes, what was it published in?

Did your story win a competition? y/n

THINGS TO DO

If yes, how much did you win? $

Who did you give copies of your story to?

Your friends | Your family | A teacher | A writer | A stranger | Other

If other, please specify

Approximately how many people have been able to read your story?

0,0,0,0,0,0,0,0,0

What was the nicest thing someone said about your story?

What was the most negative thing someone said?

How happy are you with the result?

Excellent. Your best story yet | Quite good, but you can do better | OK. Nothing special | Not good enough to be published | Terrible. You wouldn't ask anyone to read it

Start your story here

At the same time, you could complete these **Things to Do**
7: Prepare Yourself for Fame • 18: Win Something
37: Write Lyrics for a Song • 49: Read These Books

Sing in Front of an Audience

Have you noticed how many hundreds of people there are who can't sing for toffee and yet seem quite happy to display their lack of talent in front of millions of TV viewers on shows like *American Idol*? It's all about self-belief (or being tone deaf). Record yourself and play it back to get a true idea of how good you are. Then find an appropriate way to showcase your vocal abilities.

Sing When You're Winning

- If you have a good voice, don't hide it in the shower. Get involved in a local or school concert, musical, or open-mic night, and Start a Band (**Thing to Do** No. 58)—share your gift! Try to develop your talent too with singing lessons. When you're as good as you can be, it's time to decide if you want to have a go at the big time. Enter yourself into talent competitions, especially where you could get to sing on TV and get talent-spotted.
- If you think you have a terrible voice, you probably do. The only way to persuade people to let you sing in front of them is to disguise your voice by [a] allowing it to be drowned out by others (e.g., in a choir), [b] making it sound so bad it actually turns into entertainment for other people to laugh at you (e.g., on an *American Idol*–style show or doing karaoke), and [c] not actually singing at all, but lip-synching to someone else's voice.

 TV talent shows may have helped to launch Justin's, Britney's, and Christina's careers, but they rarely bring long-lasting success. For most people it takes not only talent but years of hard work and determination to build a singing career, so it's a good idea to start young!

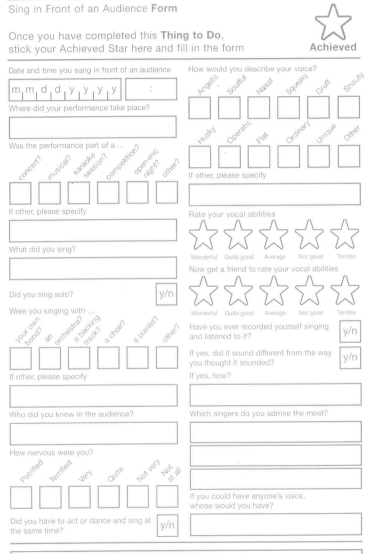

Sing in Front of an Audience **Form**

Once you have completed this **Thing to Do**,
stick your Achieved Star here and fill in the form

Achieved

Date and time you sang in front of an audience

m m d d y y y y   :

Where did your performance take place?

Was the performance part of a ...

concert?   musical?   karaoke session?   competition?   open-mic night?   other?

If other, please specify

What did you sing?

Did you sing solo?   y/n

Were you singing with ...

your own band?   an orchestra?   a backing track?   a choir?   a pianist?   other?

If other, please specify

Who did you know in the audience?

How nervous were you?

Petrified   Terrified   Very   Quite   Not very   Not at all

Did you have to act or dance and sing at the same time?   y/n

How would you describe your voice?

Angelic   Soulful   Nasal   Squeaky   Gruff   Shouty

Husky   Operatic   Flat   Ordinary   Unique   Other

If other, please specify

Rate your vocal abilities

Wonderful   Quite good   Average   Not good   Terrible

Now get a friend to rate your vocal abilities

Wonderful   Quite good   Average   Not good   Terrible

Have you ever recorded yourself singing and listened to it?   y/n

If yes, did it sound different from the way you thought it sounded?   y/n

If yes, how?

Which singers do you admire the most?

If you could have anyone's voice, whose would you have?

At the same time, you could complete these **Things to Do**
8: Learn to Play an Instrument • 37: Write Lyrics for a Song
58: Start a Band

Learn to Use Long Words (and Drop Them into Conversation)

It's embarrassing when people use words you don't know. Do you nod and pretend to understand? Stop to ask them what they mean? The worst thing you can do is not only pretend you understand, but then pop the word into conversation yourself at the risk of using it incorrectly. Well, it's time to turn the tables on the know-it-alls who scoff at your lack of literacy. Learn long difficult words and impress your family, teachers, and friends.

Discombobulate People

- Get a dictionary and skim through one letter a day, picking out a couple of attractive but tricky-looking words. Write them down in a notebook (together with a simple definition), and look at them each night before you go to sleep to help you remember them. The sooner you can use them in conversation, the better. Don't worry if you get the context a bit wrong the first time. No one will know what it means anyway.
- When you're looking for tricky words, don't go for anything so obscure that you'd have to be having a conversation about advanced quantum physics in order to get a chance to slip them in. The trick is to find words that you could use in everyday conversation.*
- If you're too embarrassed to ask someone what a word means, make a mental note of it, and as soon as you get a chance, look it up in a dictionary and add it to your "long and difficult words" list. Try it out on someone the next day. If they ask you what it means, respond with "What! Don't you know what XXXX means?"

---

*Some examples: *malapropism* (e.g., when you've used the wrong word, "Oops, I just made a malapropism.") • *postulate* (e.g., when you're asked a question, "I would postulate the answer is...") • *sententious* (e.g., when being told off, "No need to be so sententious, Dad.")

Learn to Use Long Words (and
Drop Them into Conversation) **Form**
Once you have completed this **Thing to Do**,
stick your Achieved Star here and fill in the form

☆ Achieved

Words I've heard, don't understand, and need to learn:	Long, impressive words I've learned:	Words I've completely invented (and their meaning):
_____	_____	_____
_____	_____	_____
_____	_____	_____
_____	_____	_____
_____	_____	_____
_____	_____	_____
_____	_____	_____
_____	_____	_____

When you heard these words, did you pretend to understand them? [y/n]

Did you try to use them too, even though you didn't understand them? [y/n]

If you got caught trying either of the above, what happened?

Have you dropped any of the words on this list into conversation yet? [y/n]

If yes, which ones (mark with an asterisk*)?

Who did you use them on?

What reaction did you get when you used them?

How many of these words did you invent on purpose? [0,0]

...and how many came out accidentally? [0,0]

Do you think they'll catch on? [y/n]

If you had to chose one of them to go into a dictionary, which would it be and why?

At the same time, you could complete these **Things to Do**
39: Be a Genius • 53: Succeed at Something You're Bad At
55: Invent a New Trend • 76: Learn to Say Useful Phrases in Other Languages

Blame Someone Else

There are a few things in this book you risk getting told off for. Old and boring people won't always approve of the way younger people choose to have fun. But is it right that you should be punished when your intentions are harmless? Next time someone tries to tell you off unjustly for something, do what you can to defend yourself. And if that doesn't work, you're left with only one choice: blame someone else.

It's All Your Fault

- Accidents happen. Things get broken, ruined, spilled—and then forgotten! So what's all the fuss about? They're objects, and most of the time, they're replaceable. Other things you should feel free to blame others for are losing things, being late, making the wrong decision, and forgetting things. If you have absolutely no way of proving you didn't do it—play the blame game.
- Who will you blame? Well, it's not nice to blame people you know. They won't take kindly to it either. Your best bet is to blame people who aren't there to defend themselves (e.g., strangers); those who couldn't defend themselves if they tried, because they can't talk (e.g., animals); and those who get away with causing trouble because people expect it of them or feel sorry for them (e.g., very young children).
- If you successfully get away with blaming someone else, remember to keep it a secret. You could get into double trouble for lying.

 Get off the hook: Ask a friend to back up your story or give you an alibi (say you couldn't have done it, as you were with them) • Lay on a guilt trip (e.g., "I get blamed for everything around here.") • Swear you didn't do it (keeping your fingers crossed behind your back!)

Blame Someone Else **Form**

Once you have completed this **Thing to Do**,
stick your Achieved Star here and fill in the form

Achieved

The Blame Game

What did you do (or not do)?	Who did you get into trouble with?	Who did you blame?	Did you get away with it?	If no, what happened?

At the same time, you could complete these **Things to Do**
27: Turn Back Time • **42: April Fool Someone**
89: Learn to Stick Up for Yourself • **96: Glue Coins to the Floor**

Want my lunch money? Come and get it!

Learn to Stick Up for Yourself

Everyone's been the victim of bullying at some point—even the bullies themselves. Bullying takes many different forms, and the verbal kind can be just as horrible as the physical. The bad news is that you'll come across bullies throughout your life, not just at school. The good news is that there are ways to deal with them; so the sooner you learn how, the better!

Fight for Your Right

- A lot of bullies are all talk and no action. They pick on those who look vulnerable because they're easy targets. Acting confidently makes you look more of a challenge than most bullies would care to take on. Don't provoke them, but pretend not to be scared (even if you're quaking inside). Often this will be enough to put them on edge and make them back off.
- Ignore them. Bullies are looking for a reaction, and they know the best ways to get it. But if you go against your instincts and don't respond, they'll lose interest in you soon enough.
- If you're having serious problems, tell an adult you trust enough not to do anything that will land you in even worse trouble.
- There is a saying that goes, "Defense is the best form of attack." Enroll in some self-defense classes or learn martial arts so that if you're attacked physically, you have the means to take care of yourself.
- Don't just stick up for yourself, but for others too. There's strength in numbers, and if you stand up to a bully together, they'll quickly back off.

Self-defense: There are many types of martial arts to choose from. Kung fu alone has hundreds of different styles. You could also learn karate, judo, aikido, jujitsu, kendo, tae kwon do, or kickboxing. They're fun to learn and a great way to keep fit too.

Learn to Stick Up for Yourself **Form**

Once you have completed this **Thing to Do**,
stick your Achieved Star here and fill in the form

Achieved

Certificate of Bravery

Who did you stick up for yourself in front of?

Were you alone? y/n

If no, who was with you?

How scared of this person were you before you stuck up for yourself?
Extremely / Very / Quite / A little / Not at all

Have you become less scared of them since? y/n

How have you stuck up for yourself with this person lately?
Ignored them / Pretended not to be scared / Told someone about it / Gave as good as you got / Other

How often does this person bully/attack/criticize you?
Hardly ever / From time to time / Quite often / Frequently / All the time

Describe how you used to behave when they bullied/attacked/criticized you?

How brave did you have to be to stick up for yourself?
Extremely / Very / Quite / A little / Not at all

Have you enrolled in any self-defense classes? y/n

If yes, what type of self-defense?

Do you feel more confident now?

If other, please specify

Have you ever stuck up for someone else being bullied? y/n

If yes, what happened?

Have you been bullied less since sticking up for yourself? y/n

At the same time, you could complete these **Things to Do**
14: See a Ghost • 46: Go as Fast as You Can
71: Do Something Nice without Being Asked • 80: Start Your Own Secret Society

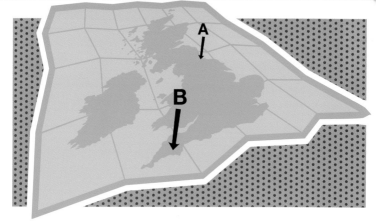

Get from A to B Using a Map

Unless you intend to spend your life hanging out in places you already know (which would be very boring), at some point you'll probably get lost. So learning how to use a map is important if you don't want to waste time going around in circles. It's great fun to explore new places—it feels like an adventure, even when you know you're not the first to have been there.

(Don't) Get Lost!

- Volunteer to do the map reading if you're being driven somewhere. It'll be easier if you keep rotating the map so it follows the direction you're traveling in (although experienced map readers may laugh at you). Keep looking ahead so that you can give the driver lots of warning before having to make a turn, or you'll soon be demoted to the backseat.
- Get a group of friends together and go exploring. You'll need a good map, a compass, a raincoat, some snacks, a charged cell phone in case you get lost and need to call for help, and a bit of spare cash for emergencies. Tell someone where you're going before you set out and let them know what time you expect to be back. The test is in not getting lost, not in seeing how fast you can go, so always stick together, waiting for slower friends to catch up.
- See if your school or a local club organizes orienteering activities. This can be done as a sport, with teams trying to find their way from A to B (and B to C, and so on) in the fastest time, or simply as a leisure activity. Either way, it's not only good fun but a great way to keep fit.

 No compass? Find out which direction the prevailing wind is blowing from before you go. Remember that the sun rises in the east and sets in the west, so shadows will point in the opposite direction. Moss tends to grow more on the north (shaded) side of tree trunks.

Get from A to B Using a Map **Form**

Once you have completed this **Thing to Do**,
stick your Achieved Star here and fill in the form

Achieved

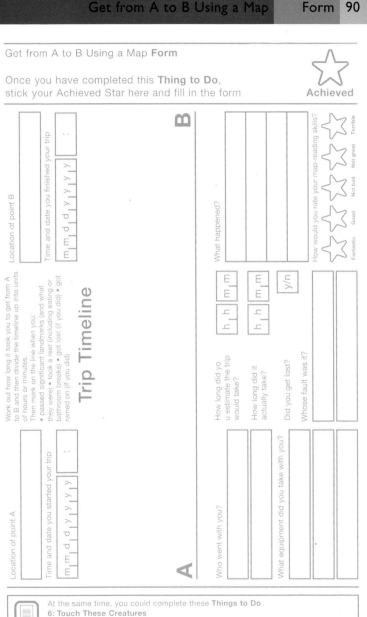

Location of point A

Time and date you started your trip

m , m , d , d , y , y , y , y   :

Trip Timeline

Work out how long it took you to get from A
to B and then divide the timeline up into units
of hours or minutes.
Then mark on the line when you:
• passed significant landmarks (and what
they were) • took a rest (including eating or
bathroom breaks) • got lost (if you did) • got
rained on (if you did)

Location of point B

Time and date you finished your trip

m , m , d , d , y , y , y , y   :

B

A

Who went with you?

What equipment did you take with you?

How long did you
estimate the trip
would take?

h , h   m , m

How long did it
actually take?

h , h   m , m

Did you get lost?

y/n

Whose fault was it?

What happened?

How would you rate your map-reading skills?

Fantastic   Good   Not bad   Not great   Terrible

At the same time, you could complete these **Things to Do**
6: Touch These Creatures
34: Hide Treasure and Leave a Map for Friends to Find

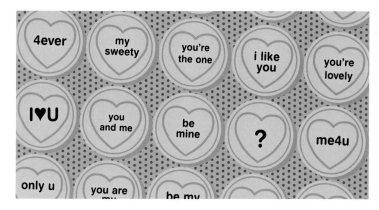

Send a Valentine Card

Is there someone you have a crush on? Well, if there is but you're too shy to tell them, February 14 provides the perfect opportunity. Whether or not you think the feeling runs both ways, send that card—it can't hurt. If nothing else, you'll make the person you like feel special. And at best, it could be the sign they were waiting for from you, and the start of a beautiful friendship. It's up to you how well you protect your identity.

S.W.A.L.K. (Sealed with a Loving Kiss)

- Make your valentine card, don't buy it—the personal touch will show how much you care. Post it if you know the boy's/girl's address. Otherwise, look for a chance to slip it into their pocket, book, or backpack without them seeing.
- Or send an e-card. They can be as anonymous as you want them to be, and there is no way they'll ever guess your handwriting!
- Don't give away who you are, but drop hints—a clue in the message, the scent of the card, the postmark. If the signs look good, you can reveal your identity. If they don't, it should be easy to convince the object of your unrequited love that you know nothing about the card.

> **Valentine Card Ideas**
>
> "Nothing takes the taste out of peanut butter quite like unrequited love"
>
> Charlie Brown
>
> * * *
>
> "Life without you is like a broken pencil...
>
> Pointless"
>
> Edmund Blackadder
>
> * * *
>
> "My heart is ever at your service"
>
> William Shakespeare

Sing a Valentine: The history of St. Valentine's Day goes back to the Romans, but the oldest known valentine card is from the 1400s and is kept in London's British Museum. Before then, valentine greetings would probably have been said or sung.

Send a Valentine Card **Form**

Once you have completed this **Thing to Do**,
stick your Achieved Star here and fill in the form

Achieved

Year you sent your card

| 0 | 2 | 1 | 4 | y | y | y | y |

Who did you send your
valentine card to?

What was your message
inside the valentine card?

Place a copy of your valentine card here

Be Mine

Did you make the card
yourself? | y/n

Did you sign your
name? | y/n

If no, did they know it
was from you? | y/n

Did you get to kiss this
person? | y/n

Did you receive a
valentine card? | y/n

If yes, who was it from?

Was it from the person
you sent your card to? | y/n

What was written inside the card you received?

At the same time, you could complete these **Things to Do**
35: Learn How to Ask Someone Out (and How to Dump Them)
77: Make Your Own Greeting Cards

I hope you like cabbages!

Have Your Own Plot in the Garden

There are many advantages to gardening: being at one with nature, out in the fresh air, getting your hands dirty. You can grow flowers and make someone's day by picking them a bunch. Learning to be self-sufficient might seem a useless skill when there are shops to buy food from, but if one day you find yourself penniless, you'll be glad you know how to grow all those vegetables you hate because they'll keep you from starving. Mind you, you'd probably Learn to Like These Foods (**Thing to Do** No. 41) much quicker if you'd grown some of them with your own fair hands.

Growing on Me

- If you don't have a garden, ask someone you know who does if you can tend a small area of theirs (they might be grateful for some help!). Alternatively, you could keep a window box or grow plants in pots.
- What will you grow? Flowers, herbs, fruit and vegetables—a tree if there's space (**Thing to Do** No. 57)? Or build a rock garden. They're good for uneven ground and tend to be quite easy to look after.
- Keep your plot separate from the rest of the garden by planting lavender or rosemary to create a border. If you plant a box hedge, you could even have a go at topiary, and cut some crazy shapes out of it.
- Grow Something from a Seed (**Thing to Do** No. 24) offers some tips on starting out. You can find lots more great gardening advice on the Internet.

 Sunflower competition: Get your friends together in the spring and each plant a sunflower seed so that come the summer you can have a competition to see whose sunflower has grown the tallest. The world-record sunflower height is over 25 ft. (7.76 m). It's been held since 1986.

Have Your Own Plot in the Garden **Form**

Once you have completed this **Thing to Do**,
stick your Achieved Star here and fill in the form

Achieved

Date you started the plot

| m | m | d | d | y | y | y | y |

Where is your plot?

In your garden | In a window box | In gardening pots | In the garden of someone you know | Other

☐ ☐ ☐ ☐ ☐

If other, please specify

How long did it take for you to see anything start to grow?

| m | m | | w | w | | d | d |

What was the first thing to appear?

How well does your garden grow?

☆ Poorly   ☆ Well   ☆ Very well   ☆ Brilliantly

How often do you garden?

Twice a week | Once a week | Once a month | When you remember to

☐ ☐ ☐ ☐

Do you tend it on your own? y/n

If no, who helps you?

What's your favorite thing in the plot?

Is your plot the best part of the garden? y/n

List the things you're growing in your plot below

How big is your plot? Write the dimensions below. Then draw in the space what you planted in your plot and where

| 0 | 0 | 0 | metres

metres

| 0 |
| 0 |

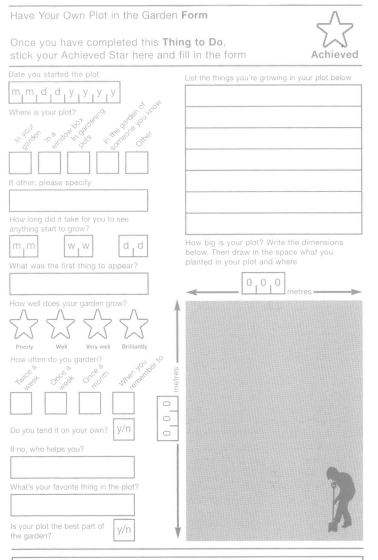

At the same time, you could complete these **Things to Do**
24: Grow Something from a Seed • **40: Take Care of an Animal** • **57: Plant a Tree (and Climb It When You're Older)** • **75: Watch a Tadpole Grow into a Frog**

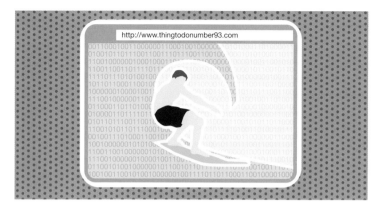

http://www.thingtodonumber93.com

Build Your Own Web Site

Anyone who is anyone has a Web site! It's the perfect place to share your knowledge or experiences with the world. You can put photos on it or write about anything that interests you—perhaps yourself! (Just take care not to put personal details like your address or phone number on there.)

Stop Surfing, Start Building

- Create a domain name. This is the address you'll find your Web site at, such as **www.101thingstodobook.com**. You will need to register your name online, but it should be fairly cheap—type "domain name" into a search engine to find the best deal. It will ask you to enter the name you want to use for your Web site, to check that no one else is using it already. If your address is unique, then you can follow the instructions for registering.
- Web space. To be able to show things on your Web site, you will need space to hold the information you want people to view. This part of the Web site will be the most costly, but there are some places that give free Web space. Type "Web space" into a search engine for a cross section of offers. The more simple your Web site, the less space you will need.
- If you've been doing the things in this book, you'll need somewhere to show your finished **Things to Do**. Upload your one-minute movie, display your T-shirt and buttons, advertise your band, launch a campaign, and keep a blog (**Things to Do** Nos. 30, 19, 47, 58, 84, and 36).
- If you get stuck and need technical advice, look on the Internet for help!

Address? The Internet works by sending packages of information. As with a package you send, each Internet "package" needs an address, or URL. If you live outside America, the last part will show which country the Web site is from (e.g., CN China, FR France, IN India).

Build Your Own Web Site **Form**

Once you have completed this **Thing to Do**,
stick your Achieved Star here and fill in the form

Achieved

Date you started your Web site

| m | m | d | d | y | y | y | y |

How long did it take to build?

| m | m | | w | w | | d | d |

Did anyone help you?

| y/n |

If yes, who?

How many hits has your site had?

| 0 | 0 | 0 | 0 | 0 | 0 | 0 | 0 |

If you have a menu on your site, list the items on it

What have you added to your site?

Photos Drawings A blog Reviews Stories Other

If other, please specify

What does your home page look like? Draw it here or place a screen grab below

Write your URL here   WWW.

At the same time, you could complete these **Things to Do**
30: **Make a One-Minute Movie** • 36: **Start Your Own Blog**
84: **Lobby Your Local Representative** • 94: **See Your Name in Print**

See Your Name in Print

You will of course be famous and legendary before too long, especially if you complete the **Things to Do** in this book. But just in case your fame is short-lived, you should have a backup plan. Get your name in print and have a permanent record of your greatness—even if it's just for rescuing your neighbor's guinea pig in a brave and heroic way.

Read All about It

- The obvious place to try to get your name in print is in the local paper. By doing something really noteworthy, you might even get a mention in the national papers. Get Your School Involved in a World Record Attempt, Win Something, Do Something Charitable, and Lobby Your Local Representative (**Things to Do** Nos. 11, 18, 43, 84) are **Things to Do** in this book that might provide perfect stories for a newspaper.
- No cheating! Placing an ad or a birthday message to your grandma in the classifieds of your local paper doesn't count! Nor does getting your name mentioned on the Internet—that's too easy.
- You could try to get something you've written/published, e.g., a story (**Thing to Do** No. 85) or an article. What's your favorite magazine? Write a review of a new film, book, or TV show, and send it in to them.
- If you know someone who is getting a book published or a CD released, try and get a mention in the dedication or the acknowledgments. If it's a book, go one better and try to get a character based on you!

Once you get a mention, frame it! It's great getting your name in print for all the world to see, but just in case someone missed it, keep a copy on your wall (and a photocopy in your pocket)—especially if you managed to get a picture of yourself printed as well.

See Your Name in Print **Form**

Once you have completed this **Thing to Do**,
stick your Achieved Star here and fill in the form

Achieved

What was the title of the publication?

What was the title of the piece you
were mentioned in?

Stick a copy of the published item here

Was there a photograph of
you too? If yes, stick it in
the space above

Date your name
appeared in print

m m d d y y y y

What did you do to get your
name in print?

How many times has
your name appeared in   0 0
print since?

How many people you
know saw your name in   0 0
print?

At the same time, you could complete these **Things to Do**
7: Prepare Yourself for Fame • 11: Get Your School Involved in a World Record
Attempt • 18: Win Something • 85: Write a Story and Get It Published

Make a Unique Milk Shake

A milk shake is an easy thing to make. All you need is a blender and ingredients that taste great together. The basic ingredients are two cups of vanilla ice cream and one cup of cold milk (use flavored milk or ice cream if you prefer)—then you can add anything you like. This will be no ordinary milk shake. You're creating the ULTIMATE milk shake. One that's so good your friends will ask you how to make it.

Great Shakes!

- Your unique milk shake will be born from trial and error. Experiment with different ingredients until you come up with a winning formula.
- The best thing is that you have to taste everything you make (although this could be a bad thing too if you're not careful about what you put in). Test your favorites on a friend to get a second opinion.
- Make sure your shake contains a special secret ingredient so that no matter how hard your friends try to recreate the shake, they can't.
- Give your milk shake creation a silly name like Banana Burp, Chockablockachocolate, or The Floaty Fruit Experience.

Ingredients to Experiment With

Whipped cream
Yogurt
Honey/Syrup
Peanut butter/Jam
Chocolate/Coffee
Toffee/Caramel
Marshmallows
Bananas
Pineapple
Strawberries
Cherries
Mango
Coconut
Cookies
Raisins
Nutella
Mint
Cinnamon
Ice
Sprinkles
Assorted sweets

 Be careful with the blender: The blades are sharp (they can even crush ice cubes if you want an extracold shake!). If someone is helping you, remember to ask them to turn away as you add the secret ingredient. Don't overmix, or your shake will be very thin.

Make a Unique Milk Shake **Form**

Once you have completed this **Thing to Do**,
stick your Achieved Star here and fill in the form

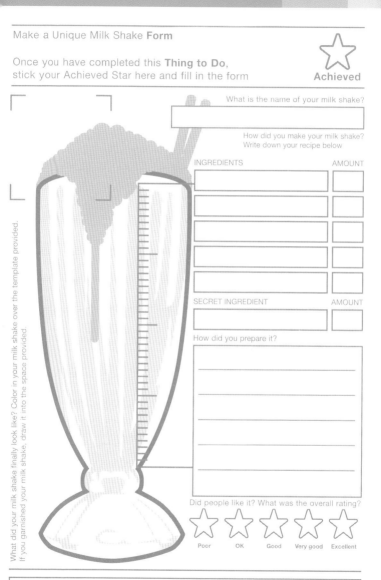

Achieved

What is the name of your milk shake?

How did you make your milk shake?
Write down your recipe below

INGREDIENTS   AMOUNT

SECRET INGREDIENT   AMOUNT

How did you prepare it?

Did people like it? What was the overall rating?

Poor   OK   Good   Very good   Excellent

What did your milk shake finally look like? Color in your milk shake over the template provided.
If you garnished your milk shake, draw it into the space provided.

At the same time, you could complete these **Things to Do**
31: Host a Party • 33: Learn to Bake a Cake
73: Have a Sleepover

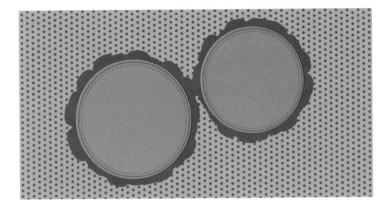

Glue Coins to the Floor

Glue coins to the floor? Why would you want to do that? Because this is a great prank. If you chose to glue fifty cents to the floor, it will be money well spent while you're entertained by all the people trying to make a fast buck but who actually only succeed in making themselves look silly and cheap.

In for a Penny, in for a Pound

- Pick a busy spot on a pavement—a spot that you can watch from a safe distance as the prank unfolds, like opposite a park. The more people walking past the better, as it increases the chance of someone spotting the coins (and their embarrassment when they fail to pick them up).*
- Have a look at what change you've got. It doesn't matter how small the value of the coins is, someone will always go for it. However, the higher in value, the more takers you'll get.
- Using an all-purpose nontoxic glue, stick your coins to the pavement. Try to do this when there's no one around, or just be very subtle. Kneel down as if you were going to tie your shoelace, and glue them while no one is looking.
- Retreat to your vantage point, sit back, and enjoy the show! If you have a camera, record people's attempts to pick up the coins. To humiliate them further, you could even broadcast your comedy on the Internet. (**Thing to Do** No. 93). Eventually, the coins will become unstuck and people will make off with your cash, but it'll have been totally worth it.

---

*The best places for the prank: In front of a shop doorway • Near an ATM • At a bus stop • In the school playground • Outside a movie theater • At the supermarket • At a subway or train station • Outside your house or your friend's house

Glue Coins to the Floor **Form**

Once you have completed this **Thing to Do**,
stick your Achieved Star here and fill in the form

Achieved

Date and time you glued coins to the floor

| m | m | d | d | y | y | y | y | | : |

Where did you glue the coins?

Why did you pick this place?

How much did you
glue to the floor?
Draw the amount in
the coins provided

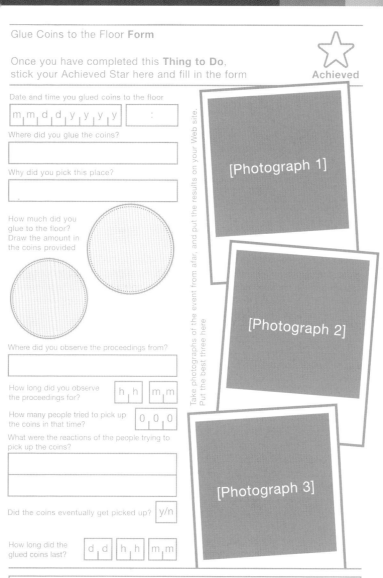

Take photographs of the event from afar, and put the results on your Web site.
Put the best three here

[Photograph 1]

[Photograph 2]

[Photograph 3]

Where did you observe the proceedings from?

How long did you observe
the proceedings for? | h | h | | m | m |

How many people tried to pick up
the coins in that time? | 0 | 0 | 0 |

What were the reactions of the people trying to
pick up the coins?

Did the coins eventually get picked up? | y/n |

How long did the
glued coins last? | d | d | | h | h | | m | m |

At the same time, you could complete these **Things to Do**
42: April Fool Someone • 74: Become a Spy
88: Blame Someone Else

Learn to Take Great Photos

With cameras becoming ever smaller and more portable, and most cell phones having one, there's no excuse for not taking lots of photos documenting the exciting life you're leading now in case you become old and boring and need to survive on good memories. What do you want to take pictures of?

Say Cheese

- Always have a camera on hand (and a steady hand at that!) to snap something that catches your eye. The greatest photos tell stories, but they may still have been taken on the spur of the moment. Find new ways of looking at everyday scenes, and pay attention to life's smallest details.
- Composition—the position of different elements within the photo—is very important. Check that the background and foreground aren't interfering with one another (e.g., a tree growing out of someone's head) or that you're not cutting important things off (such as the head itself!).
- Your composition doesn't have to be balanced, so don't assume your subject has to be centered. Look for natural ways of framing the shot and drawing the eye to the subject. People and animals often tell stories with their faces, so don't be afraid to let them fill the frame.
- Lighting and color will affect the mood, just as it does in a painting. Tilt the camera to see things from interesting angles and create drama.
- If you want to take photos of animals, you'll need tons of patience. You also need to know your subject well so that you can predict its behavior.

Landscapes are hard to pull off—photos tend to flatten and shrink scenery. Make sure your photo has a foreground, background, and middle ground, adding depth to the shot. Dramatic variety in light and shade will also help, so take photos when the sun is low.

Learn to Take Great Photos **Form**

Once you have completed this **Thing to Do**,
stick your Achieved Star here and fill in the form

Achieved

Place your favorite
animal photograph
that you've taken here

Date and time of the photograph

| m | m | d | d | y | y | y | y | | : |

What is your title for this photograph?

Place your favorite
family or friends photograph
that you've taken here

Date and time of the photograph

| m | m | d | d | y | y | y | y | | : |

What is your title for this photograph?

Place your favorite
landscape photograph
that you've taken here

Date and time of the photograph

| m | m | d | d | y | y | y | y | | : |

What is your title for this photograph?

Place your all-time
favorite photograph
that you've taken here

Date and time of the photograph

| m | m | d | d | y | y | y | y | | : |

What is your title for this photograph?

At the same time, you could complete these **Things to Do**
12: Paint a Picture Good Enough to Hang on the Wall
30: Make a One-Minute Movie • 32: Visit...

Drive Something

If you thought you'd have to content yourself with bumper cars and remote-control cars until you passed your driving test, think again. Under super-vision and wearing the right safety equipment, you can drive all sorts of engine-powered vehicles, so long as you don't drive them on public roads or footpaths. To do that, you do need a licence, or you're breaking the law!

Easy Riders

- **ATV (All Terrain Vehicles):** If you want to experience different kinds of terrain, go to the countryside and get on an ATV. Rental centers offer driving and safety lessons as well as use of their equipment and tracks.
- **Go-Cart:** This is for those of you with a fierce competitive spirit. Pretend you're a Formula-1 driver and race your family and friends around a track. There are indoor and outdoor tracks across the U.S.
- **Motorcycle:** It's a very expensive hobby, but if your parents can afford to buy you a dirt bike then there's a world of motorcycle sport, like motocross, for you to discover.
- **Racing games:** OK, it's not really driving, but it's close, and if you can't afford the real thing, then some games can be a good second best. In some ways, they're better than racing the real thing—you can go much faster and it doesn't matter if you crash. Visit an arcade and race your friends, or if you're playing at home, make sure you use a steering wheel instead of a keyboard or joystick to make it more realistic.

Old MacDonald had a tractor: If you know someone who owns a farm, ask them nicely if you can have a go on their tractor. Obviously you'll have to be supervised, as the farmer won't want squashed wheat or ploughed chicken. Neither will the chickens!

Drive Something **Form**

Once you have completed this **Thing to Do**,
stick your Achieved Star here and fill in the form

Achieved

ATV

Date you drove

m , m , d , d , y , y , y , y

What was the terrain like?

☐ Forest ☐ Sand ☐ Mud ☐ Hills ☐ Road

How powerful was the ATV?

How difficult was it to drive?

☐ Very ☐ Quite ☐ A little ☐ Not very ☐ Not at all

What was your max speed? 0 , 0 , 0 mph

Go Cart

Date you drove

m , m , d , d , y , y , y , y

How many people did you race against? 0 , 0

Did you win a race? y/n

If no, what was your best finishing position?

What was your worst finishing position?

How difficult was it to drive?

☐ Very ☐ Quite ☐ A little ☐ Not very ☐ Not at all

What was your max speed? 0 , 0 , 0 mph

Motorcycle

Date you drove

m , m , d , d , y , y , y , y

Where were you?

What kind of bike was it?

How powerful was the bike?

Was it a race? y/n

How difficult was it to drive?

☐ Very ☐ Quite ☐ A little ☐ Not very ☐ Not at all

What was your max speed? 0 , 0 , 0 mph

Other

Date you drove

m , m , d , d , y , y , y , y

What did you drive?

Where were you?

Was it a race? y/n

If yes, did you win?

How difficult was it to drive?

☐ Very ☐ Quite ☐ A little ☐ Not very ☐ Not at all

What was your max speed? 0 , 0 , 0 mph

At the same time, you could complete these **Things to Do**
18: Win Something • 46: Go As Fast As You Can
61: Join a Club

Thank you

Be Vegetarian for a Week

For a week, try replacing beef, ham, and chicken with stuffed peppers, yummy stir-fries, or vegetable lasagna. Vegetarianism isn't all about lentils and salad, and if you aren't a convert to vegetarianism after your experimental week, at least you will have realized how tasty food without meat can be.

Food for Thought

- Only eat what you feel comfortable with. You don't have to like everything. If you're finding it really hard, then try something with a meat substitute—there are lots of tasty ones around.
- When you eat somewhere other than home, warn whoever's catering that you're not eating meat. Don't be afraid to ask if a dish is vegetarian.
- Being vegetarian isn't always a choice. Some people can become intolerant of certain foods at any time and have to resort to being vegetarian.
- If you do decide to go "veggie," it's important to make sure you still eat foods that, combined, have similar nutrients to meat: like whole grains, nuts, green vegetables, and soy.

Types of Vegetarian

A **pesco vegetarian** diet excludes meat and poultry but includes fish, dairy products, and egg. Many would argue that this does not make it vegetarian at all.

A **lacto vegetarian** diet excludes meat, fish, poultry, and egg but includes dairy products.

An **ovo vegetarian** diet excludes meat, fish, poultry, and dairy products but includes egg.

A **lacto-ovo vegetarian** diet excludes meat, fish, and poultry but includes dairy products and egg.

A **vegan** diet excludes meat, fish, poultry, egg, and dairy products. Most vegans take this further and refuse to use anything made with animal products, including silk, leather, wool, etc.

Vegetarianism was practiced in Egypt around 3,200 BC due to beliefs in reincarnation. Hinduism and Buddhism also encourage it. Many famous Greek philosophers, like Plato, Socrates, Pythagoras, and Aristotle, were vegetarians who were against animal cruelty.

Be Vegetarian for a Week **Form**

Once you have completed this **Thing to Do**,
stick your Achieved Star here and fill in the form

☆ Achieved

Name your least favorite meal

Do you think you might continue being veggie? y/n

Name one new thing you liked

Did you feel better for giving up meat? y/n

Name your favorite meal

Did you cheat at all? y/n

Date you started
m m d d y y y y

Did you find it hard to be veggie for a week? y/n

Your veggie menu

Monday

Tuesday

Wednesday

Thursday

Friday

Saturday

Sunday

At the same time, you could complete these **Things to Do**
41: **Learn to Like These Foods**
60: **Learn to Live without Something You Love for a Week**

BECKHAM
7

To _____ from
David Beckham

Meet Someone Famous

To achieve this **Thing to Do**, you need to meet a true A-list celebrity. This means a Hollywood star (no soap stars), an international pop star (their drummer doesn't count, nor does the member of some fly-by-night boy or girl band), a Nobel-prize winner, and anyone else who has an international reputation, be it in writing, sports, politics, or business. Have a pen and paper for an autograph and a camera with you when you're celebrity-hunting.

Don't You Know Who I Am?

- Find out about movie premieres through the Internet and film magazines. Arrive early to get in the front row and call to the stars as they pass by. Also hang around stage doors of theaters and concert venues, enter competitions where the prize is to meet somebody famous (**Thing to Do** No. 18), and Take Part in a TV Show (**Thing to Do** No. 68).
- You don't want to sound crazy or stupid when you meet them. Rather than gush, how about a bit of constructive criticism (e.g., "I liked you in X, but I thought you could have been a bit more…")? If you meet a famous person you don't respect highly, pretend you don't know who they are. They'll either be offended or relieved to have retained some anonymity. Of course, if you get all starry-eyed, words might fail you altogether.
- Whatever happens, get that autograph or photo to prove you met them. Ask them for something from their pockets too—anything at all. When you sell it on eBay it could be worth a small fortune.

Celebrity-hunting tips: Read gossip magazines and fan Web sites to find out where the rich and famous are hanging out. For random celebrity-hunting, try expensive department stores like Bergdorf Goodman and Barneys and designer clothes shops. Airports are good places too.

Meet Someone Famous **Form**

Once you have completed this **Thing to Do**,
stick your Achieved Star here and fill in the form

Achieved

Date and time you met someone famous

| m | m | d | d | y | y | y | y | | : |

Did they let you take a photograph
of the two of you together? If yes,
place the photograph below

Who did you meet?

Was your meeting ...

By chance? [ ]   Engineered by you? [ ]

Where were you when you met them?

How long did you spend with them?

| h | h | | m | m | | s | s |

Were they as you expected them to be? [y/n]

If no, why not?

You and _____

Were they friendly? [y/n]

What did you get from your celebrity?

Sweet nothing [ ]   A smile [ ]   A handshake [ ]   An autograph [ ]   Something from their pocket [ ]   Other [ ]

If other, please specify

What did you say to the celebrity?

Ask the celebrity to sign their name here

What did they say to you?

At the same time, you could complete these **Things to Do**
68: Take Part in a TV Show
72: See Your Music Idol Perform Live

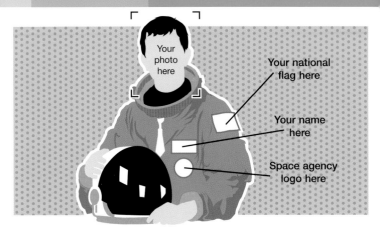

Your photo here

Your national flag here

Your name here

Space agency logo here

Decide What You Want to Be When You Grow Up

This **Thing to Do** isn't about what you think you will or won't be able to do when you leave school. It's about what you want to do. Everyone needs a dream or ambition, no matter how unrealistic it might seem. Perhaps you've known what you wanted to do from the age of three when you first picked up that hairbrush and sung along to Kylie, or kicked a ball around the garden. However, if you haven't found your niche in life yet, don't worry—there's plenty of time. Relax, shut your eyes, and dream away...

I Want It All

- Don't let others tell you that you can't do something or pressure you into a career you don't want. Pursue your dream regardless of financial rewards or whether or not you think you're good at it. Hard work, patience, and passion will get you far. A third of our waking adult lives is spent at work—that's a lot of time wasted if you're unhappy in your job. Surely it's better to try to achieve your dream even if you don't ever quite make it, than spend your life wondering, "What if...?"
- Few successful people get to be where they are without a bit of luck and being in the right place at the right time. Look out for and seize any opportunities that offer even a remote chance of moving you a step closer to your dream. Make things happen!
- Once you've decided what you want to do, start planning how you're going to achieve it. Seek advice from those who have made it.

Dream job ideas: Actor • Artist • Astronaut • Brain surgeon • Chef • Comedian • Dancer Detective • Fighter pilot • Film director • Inventor • Model • Musician • Poet • Politician Scientist • Singer • Athlete • Spy • Superhero • TV star • Vet • Writer

Decide What You Want to Be When You Grow Up **Form**

Once you have completed this **Thing to Do**,
stick your Achieved Star here and fill in the form

Achieved

Write your dream job here

What are the best things about this job?

Name three things you can do over the next few
years to prepare yourself for this career

What skills do you need for this job?

Name three people you admire who do this job

What sort of qualifications do you think you
might need?

Name three other jobs you'd like to do

How would you rate your chances of getting a
job like this?

Very good   Optimistic   OK   Not good   Terrible

If you don't think your chances are good,
explain why not

Come back to this book in 20 years
and fill in the section below

For future use

Did you get your dream job?   y/n

If yes, is it everything you'd
hoped it would be?   y/n

If no, what job do you do instead?

At the same time, you could complete these **Things to Do**
7: Prepare Yourself for Fame • 38: Make a Time Capsule
39: Be a Genius • 53: Succeed at Something You're Bad At

Appendix

In the following pages are items to help you get more out of your
101 Things to Do Before You're Old and Boring book

Your **Things to Do**

A list for you to fill in with any **Things to Do** that weren't mentioned in
the book but that you think should be included.

Write Your Own **Thing to Do**

After you've written a list of your own **Things to Do**, turn over to find
two more pages designed for you to write about one of them in the style
of the other **Things to Do** in this book.

- Once you've completed your **Thing to Do**, write the results in the
  space provided. Make your own form, including dates, descriptions, and
  other details of interest.
- If you disagree with any of our **Things to Do**, cut out and place your
  new **Thing to Do** over an existing one that you know you'll never
  complete.

Pocket-Sized Checklist

A handy checklist to keep with you all the time. Compare yours with
your friends' and use it to check **Things to Do** off the minute you've
completed them.

Extra Paper

Photocopy the extra pages if you run out of space on a form, and use
them to continue writing. When you're done, attach them to the
relevant form.

Acknowledgments

A thank you to all the people who have helped to make this book
possible.

About the Authors

Who are we, and what do we do?

Your Things to Do

List the **Things to Do** that you'd like to do before you're old and boring that weren't mentioned in the book

Thing to Do 1

Thing to Do 2

Thing to Do 3

Thing to Do 4

Thing to Do 5

Thing to Do 6

Thing to Do 7

Thing to Do 8

Thing to Do 9

Thing to Do 10

Enter your favorite **Thing to Do** that wasn't mentioned in the book into the next spread

Title for Your **Thing to Do**

Choose a **Thing to Do** that you'd like to complete but that wasn't featured in the book. Write a description of your **Thing to Do** and how to do it and paste it over this text.

Draw in the space provided above, an illustration relating to your **Thing to Do**. Place the title for your **Thing to Do** in the yellow bar at the top and decide which category it should fit into: Adventure, Mischief, Create, Family and Friends, Hobbies, Nature, Pets and Animals, Fame and Fortune, Learn to..., Sport and Activity, Miscellaneous, or Make a Difference.

On the right-hand side, design a form and fill it in with the details of what happened when you completed your **Thing to Do**.

Other Possible **Things to Do**

- Learn to Dance
- Start Your Autobiography
- Discover the Meaning of Life
- Invent the Funniest Joke Ever
- Eat Something That's Still Alive
- Rule the World

Interesting Fact
Write an interesting fact about your Thing to Do in this space provided.

Once you have written your **Thing to Do**, stick
your Achieved Star here and design your own form

Achieved

How to Use Your Pocket-Sized Checklist

Use the following instructions to keep track of your
completed **Things to Do** at a moment's notice

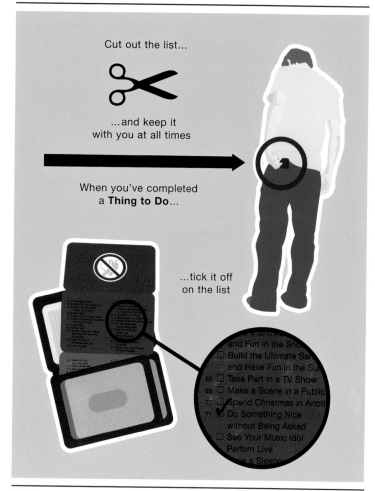

Cut out the list...

...and keep it
with you at all times

When you've completed
a **Thing to Do**...

...tick it off
on the list

and Fun in the Sno
☐ Build the Ultimate Sa
and Have Fun in the Su
68 ☐ Take Part in a TV Show
69 ☐ Make a Scene in a Public
70 ☐ Spend Christmas in Anoth
71 ☑ Do Something Nice
without Being Asked
☐ See Your Music Idol
Perform Live
ve a Sleepo

Small print: Keep this list with you at all times. Use every opportunity to complete the **Things to Do** on this list.

1 □ Send a Message in a Bottle
2 □ Run up an Escalator the Wrong Way
3 □ Make an Origami Crane
4 □ Learn How to Tell When Someone Likes You
5 □ Keep a Dream Diary
6 □ Touch These Creatures
7 □ Prepare Yourself for Fame
8 □ Learn to Play an Instrument
9 □ Play a Computer Game to the End
10 □ Have an Embarrassing Moment and Get over It
11 □ Get Your School Involved in a World Record Attempt

12 □ Paint a Picture Good Enough to Hang on the Wall
13 □ Learn to Whistle (and Make Other Noises)
14 □ See a Ghost
15 □ Fart and Burp
16 □ Make a Swear Box
17 □ Act in a Play
18 □ Win Something
19 □ Make a T-shirt
20 □ Stay Up All Night
21 □ Sleep All Day
22 □ Invent a Secret Code
23 □ Learn to Do a Card Trick
24 □ Grow Something from a Seed

Checklist

25 ☐ Start a Collection
26 ☐ Help Save the Planet
27 ☐ Turn Back Time
28 ☐ Learn to Do a Party Trick
29 ☐ Climb to the Top of a Mountain
30 ☐ Make a One-Minute Movie
31 ☐ Host a Party
32 ☐ Visit...
33 ☐ Learn to Bake a Cake
34 ☐ Hide a Treasure and Leave a
Map for Friends to Find
35 ☐ Learn How to Ask Someone Out
(and How to Dump Them)
36 ☐ Start Your Own Blog
37 ☐ Write Lyrics for a Song
38 ☐ Make a Time Capsule
39 ☐ Be a Genius

40 ☐ Take Care of an Animal
41 ☐ Learn to Like These Foods
42 ☐ April Fool Someone
43 ☐ Do Something Charitable
44 ☐ Teach Your Grandparents
Something New
45 ☐ Invent a New Game
46 ☐ Go as Fast as You Can
47 ☐ Make Your Own Buttons
48 ☐ Watch These Films
49 ☐ Read These Books
50 ☐ Pretend to Be Sick Convincingly
51 ☐ Save Your Allowance for a Month
and Spend It All at Once
52 ☐ Learn to Swim
53 ☐ Succeed at Something You're Bad At
54 ☐ Be a Daredevil

55 ☐ Invent a New Trend
56 ☐ Know Who Your Friends Are
57 ☐ Plant a Tree (and Climb
It When You're Older)
58 ☐ Start a Band
59 ☐ Camp Out in the Backyard
60 ☐ Learn to Live without Something
You Love for a Week
61 ☐ Join a Club
62 ☐ Cook a Meal
63 ☐ List the Things Your Parents
Say They'll Tell You When
You're Older
64 ☐ Make Your Bike or
Skateboard Look Cool
65 ☐ Learn to Juggle

66 ☐ Have a Snowball Fight
and Fun in the Snow
67 ☐ Build the Ultimate Sandcastle
and Have Fun in the Sun
68 ☐ Take Part in a TV Show
69 ☐ Make a Scene in a Public Place
70 ☐ Spend Christmas in Another Country
71 ☐ Do Something Nice
without Being Asked
72 ☐ See Your Music Idol
Perform Live
73 ☐ Have a Sleepover
74 ☐ Become a Spy
75 ☐ Watch a Tadpole Grow
into a Frog
76 ☐ Learn to Say Useful Phrases
in Other Languages

77 ☐ Make Your Own
Greeting Cards
78 ☐ Hold a Garage Sale
79 ☐ Build an Igloo
80 ☐ Start Your Own Secret Society
81 ☐ Research Your Family Tree
82 ☐ Learn to Skip Stones
83 ☐ Dye Your Hair
84 ☐ Lobby Your Local Representative
85 ☐ Write a Story and Get It Published
86 ☐ Sing in Front of an Audience
87 ☐ Learn to Use Long Words
(and Drop Them into Conversation)
88 ☐ Blame Someone Else

89 ☐ Learn to Stick Up for Yourself
90 ☐ Get from A to B Using a Map
91 ☐ Send a Valentine Card
92 ☐ Have Your Own Plot in the Garden
93 ☐ Build Your Own Web Site
94 ☐ See Your Name in Print
95 ☐ Make a Unique Milk Shake
96 ☐ Glue Coins to the Floor
97 ☐ Learn to Take Great Photos
98 ☐ Drive Something
99 ☐ Be Vegetarian for a Week
100 ☐ Meet Someone Famous
101 ☐ Decide What You Want to
Be When You Grow Up

Write the name of the **Thing to Do** title here

Cut here

Cut here

Extra Paper

Write the name of the **Thing to Do** title here

Cut here

Cut here